Janice VanCleave's

The Human Body for Every Kid

Other Books by Janice VanCleave

Science for Every Kid series:
  Janice VanCleave's Astronomy for Every Kid
  Janice VanCleave's Biology for Every Kid
  Janice VanCleave's Chemistry for Every Kid
  Janice VanCleave's Dinosaurs for Every Kid
  Janice VanCleave's Earth Science for Every Kid
  Janice VanCleave's Geography for Every Kid
  Janice VanCleave's Geometry for Every Kid
  Janice VanCleave's Math for Every Kid
  Janice VanCleave's Physics for Every Kid

Spectacular Science Projects series:
  Janice VanCleave's Animals
  Janice VanCleave's Earthquakes
  Janice VanCleave's Electricity
  Janice VanCleave's Gravity
  Janice VanCleave's Machines
  Janice VanCleave's Magnets
  Janice VanCleave's Microscopes and Magnifying Lenses
  Janice VanCleave's Molecules
  Janice VanCleave's Volcanoes

Janice VanCleave's

The Human Body for Every Kid

Easy Activities that Make Learning Science Fun

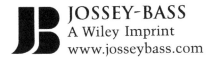

JOSSEY-BASS
A Wiley Imprint
www.josseybass.com

Published by Jossey-Bass
A Wiley Imprint
989 Market Street, San Francisco, CA 94103-1741   www.josseybass.com

Design and production by: WordCrafters Editorial Services, Inc.
Illustrator: Laurel Aiello

Jossey-Bass books and products are available through most bookstores. To contact Jossey-Bass directly call our Customer Care Department within the U.S. at 800-956-7739, outside the U.S. at 317-572-3986, or fax 317-572-4002.

Jossey-Bass also publishes its books in a variety of electronic formats. Some content that appears in print may not be available in electronic books.

Library of Congress Cataloging-in-Publication Data

VanCleave, Janice Pratt.
    Janice VanCleave's the human body for every kid   :   easy activities
that make learning science fun.
        p.   cm.
    Includes index.
    ISBN 0-471-02413-9—ISBN 0-471-02408-2 (pbk.)
    1. Human physiology—Experiments—Juvenile Literature. [1. Human
physiology—Experiments. 2. Body, Human—Experiments.
3. Experiments.] I. Title. II. Title: Human body for every kid.
QP37.V36   1995
612'.078—dc20   94-20862
                                                                                                              AC

Printed in the United States of America
FIRST EDITION
PB Printing   10

The adults listed here are all part of the staff at John Wiley & Sons, Inc.: Estelle Conklin, Tom Conter, PJ Dempsey, Chris Jackson, Dean Karrel, Stephen Kippur, Judith McCarthy, Nana Prior, Kara Raezer, Marcia Samuels, George Stanley, Deborah Wiley, and Peter Wiley.

These adults are related to a special group of children whose names are not only listed below, but are found printed in the art throughout this book. I hope they have fun performing the experiments and take special pride in the one containing their name.

It is my pleasure to dedicate this book to the following young budding scientists. Joshua Anderson, Joey and Morgan Conklin, Meghann Conter, Courtney Dempsey, Katherine McCarthy Gelinne, Melissa and Scott Karrel, Sabrina and Sara Kippur, Johnny and Julie Raezer, Christina and Margitta Rogers, Claire and Richard Samuels, Alison and Christopher Stanley, Andrew and Elizabeth Wiley, Beau and Nate Wiley.

Contents

Introduction

This book is about a very special animal found all over the earth. This animal is like other animals in many ways. It must have regular supplies of food, water, and oxygen to live. But while this animal needs an environment with these life-supporting materials, it also has been observed in places without them, such as on the surface of the earth's moon and deep within the waters of the earth's oceans.

How does this animal manage to survive in different environments? Unlike other animals, it can observe its surroundings, identify problems, come up with solutions to problems, test ideas, and evaluate the results. In other words, this unique animal has the mental capabilities to use the scientific method to learn more about itself and the world around it.

Have you guessed that this book is all about . . . *you*? Yes, this is a book about the human body. It is a study of **anatomy**, the parts of the human body and their functions.

No two people are exactly alike. They differ in many ways, such as body shape, height, skin color, hair color, and facial features. These differences make you the unique person that you are. But, even though no one is exactly like you, every human being has the same basic anatomy. The information in this book is about a typical person. Your body may differ slightly from the descriptions and drawings.

It seems that we have always been interested in what makes our body function. The earliest scientists, called natural philosophers, believed that through investigation one could discover how the natural processes of the human body work.

Aristotle (384–322 B.C.) was one of the greatest natural philosophers, but he thought the heart was the source from which all sensations originated. Unlike later authorities on the human body, such as Claudius Galen (A.D. 130–200) and Andreas Vesalius (1514–1564), Aristotle and other scientists of his day observed but did not experiment. While Galen was for centuries considered the greatest authority on the human body, he learned about the human body only by studying the bodies of monkeys. Vesalius, considered the father of modern anatomy, was the first to actually study the inside of the human body and write a human anatomy textbook.

As time passed, each generation gathered new information, slowly accumulating more knowledge about the human body. The wonderful fact that there is still so very much to learn and understand should excite all young scientists and encourage them to seek answers to unsolved problems and to question things presented as fact.

This book provides fun experiments that teach known concepts about the human body. It is designed to teach facts, concepts, and problem-solving strategies. The scientific concepts presented can be applied to many similar situations. The exercises and activities were selected for their ability to be explained in basic terms with little complexity. One of the main objectives of the book is to present the *fun* of science.

How to Use This Book

Read each of the 25 sections slowly and follow all procedures carefully. You will learn best if each section is read in order, as there is some buildup of information as the book progresses. The format for each section is as follows:

- The chapter subtitle identifies the focus of the chapter.

- **What You Need to Know:** A definition and explanation of facts you need to understand.

- **Exercises:** To help you apply the facts you have learned.
- **Activity:** A project related to the facts represented.
- **Solutions to Exercises:** With a step-by-step explanation of the thought process.

In addition, this book contains:

- **Glossary:** The first time a term is introduced in the book, it will be **boldfaced** and defined in the text. The term and definition are also included in the Glossary at the end of the book. Be sure to flip back to the Glossary as often as you need to, making each term part of your personal vocabulary.

General Instructions for the Exercises

1. Read the exercise carefully. If you are not sure of the answers, reread What You Need to Know for clues.

2. Check your answers against those in the Solutions and evaluate your work.

3. Do the exercise again if any of your answers is incorrect.

General Instructions for the Activities

1. Read the activity completely before starting.

2. Collect supplies. You will have less frustration and more fun if all the materials necessary for the activity are ready before you start. You lose your train of thought when you have to stop and search for supplies.

3. Do not rush through the activity. Follow each step very carefully; never skip steps, and do not add your own. Safety is of the utmost importance, and by reading each activity before starting, then following the instructions exactly, you can feel confident that no unexpected results will occur.

4. Observe. If your results are not the same as those described in the activity, carefully reread the instructions and start over from step 1.

1
Building Blocks
Parts and Functions of Living Cells

What You Need to Know

In 1665, the English scientist Robert Hooke (1635–1703) made a startling discovery. While studying a slice of cork under a microscope, he saw that the cork was made up of tiny, empty cavities (holes) enclosed by what looked like walls. The holes looked to Hooke like the small rooms, or "cells," in a monastery. Thus, he named the structures he had found **cells** (the smallest units, or the building blocks, of all living things).

In 1839, two German biologists working separately, Matthias Schleiden and Theodor Schwann, discovered that all living things are made up of cells. At this time it was known that cells are not actually empty. Instead they are filled with a jellylike material. The work of Schleiden and Schwann and others established what is known as the **cell theory**, which states that (1) all living things are made up of cells and (2) all cells come from previously existing cells.

As the microscope has improved through the years, many cell structures and their functions have been identified. The diagram shown here illustrates basic cell structure. Each part of the cell has a specific function, as described below.

1. **Cell membrane:** The thin filmlike outer layer that holds the cell together and separates it from its environment. It allows materials to pass into and out of the cell.

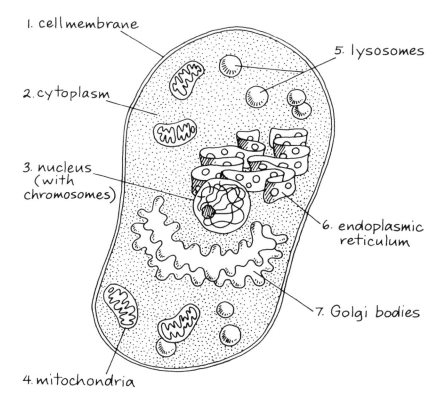

1. cell membrane
2. cytoplasm
3. nucleus (with chromosomes)
4. mitochondria
5. lysosomes
6. endoplasmic reticulum
7. Golgi bodies

2. **Cytoplasm:** A jellylike material made mostly of water. It fills the cell, and the other parts of the cell float in it.

3. **Nucleus:** The control center that directs all the activities of the cell. It is shaped like a sphere and contains **chromosomes**, which are special threadlike structures that carry instructions, much like a computer program, to make the cell work.

4. **Mitochondria:** The cell's power stations, where food and oxygen react to produce the energy needed for the cell to work and live.

5. **Lysosomes:** The parts of the cell that contain chemicals used to destroy harmful substances or worn-out cell parts.

6. **Endoplasmic reticulum:** The structure within the cell where protein is made. Protein is used for growth and repair.

7. **Golgi bodies:** The structure within the cell where proteins are stored until needed.

Your body contains trillions of cells. Each cell has a job to perform, and all cells must work together to keep you alive and well. A group of similar cells that perform a special job form **tissue**, such as skin, nerve, muscle, and bone tissue. Different tissues working together form **organs**, such as your heart and lungs. A group of different organs working together to perform a particular job forms a **system**, such as the circulatory or respiratory system. All the systems working together in a living being form an **organism**, such as you.

Cells come in different shapes and sizes, depending on the special job that they perform. Muscle cells are long and can shorten or lengthen to allow you to move. Nerve cells have long fibers that send messages around your body. Red blood cells are disk shaped and able to transport oxygen.

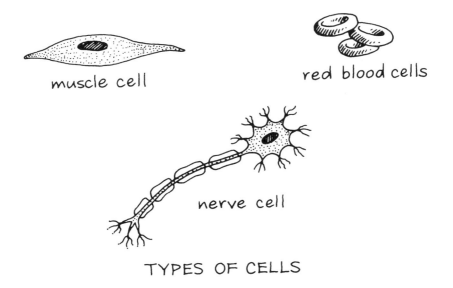

muscle cell

red blood cells

nerve cell

TYPES OF CELLS

Most cells are too small to see with the unaided eye. The **ovum** (female sex cell, or egg) is the largest human body cell, with a diameter of about 0.008 inches (0.02 cm). The smallest cells in the body, with diameters of about 0.0002 inches (0.0005 cm), are found in your brain.

Exercise

Cells in your body live for different amounts of time. Bone cells can last for many years, while cells lining your small intestine live for only a few days. Cells die in your body every second, but new cells are constantly being made to replace them. New cells are made when a cell divides into two identical new cells. The steps showing how cells reproduce to make new cells are listed below. Match each step with the diagram that represents it.

1. One cell.

2. The cell grows larger.

3. The nucleus starts to divide.

4. The cell membrane starts to break apart.

5. Two new identical cells.

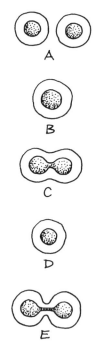

Activity: WORLD-CLASS CELL MODEL

Purpose To construct a model that shows three parts of a cell.

Materials lemon gelatin dessert mix
1-pint (125-ml) resealable plastic bag
quart (liter) bowl
large grape
adult helper

Procedure

1. Have your adult helper mix the ingredients for the gelatin dessert according to the instructions on the box.

2. Allow the gelatin to cool to room temperature.

3. Pour the gelatin into the resealable bag, seal the bag, and place it in the bowl.

4. Set the bowl and bag in the refrigerator and chill until the gelatin is firm (about 3 to 4 hours).

5. Remove the gelatin from the refrigerator and open the bag.

6. Using your finger, insert the grape into the center of the gelatin.

7. Reseal the bag.

8. Place the bag of gelatin on a flat surface such as the kitchen counter. Observe its shape.

9. Hold the bag over the bowl as you gently squeeze it. (The bowl is used in the event that you squeeze too hard and the bag opens.) Observe the shape of the bag as you squeeze.

Results A model of a cell with three parts is made. Squeezing the model or placing it on a hard surface causes its shape to change.

Why?   All the cells in your body, like the model, have these three parts: a cell membrane, cytoplasm, and a nucleus. The plastic bag, like a cell membrane, keeps the parts of the cell together and acts as a barrier to protect the inner parts. The pale color of the gelatin dessert simulates the grayish jellylike material, called cytoplasm, that fills the cell. It is in the cytoplasm that most of the chemical work of the cell takes place. Floating in the gelatin is a grape that represents the nucleus, the cell's governing body. The cell membrane, cytoplasm, and nucleus all work together and are necessary for the life of the cell. Most of the cells in your body, like the model, change shape when pressure is applied. Bone cells are more rigid and keep their shape.

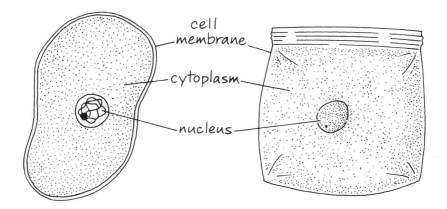

Solutions to Exercises

1. *Think!*

   • Both diagrams B and D show a single cell.

   • Which diagram, B or D, represents the cell before it starts to enlarge?

   Step 1 matches diagram D.

2. *Think!*

   • The enlarged single cell is diagram B.

   Step 2 matches diagram B.

3. *Think!*

   • The nucleus is a sphere in the center of the cell.

   • Both diagrams C and E show the nucleus dividing, but which diagram shows the nucleus just starting to divide?

   Step 3 matches diagram C.

4. *Think!*

   • As the cell membrane starts to break apart, it gets narrower in the middle.

   • Which diagram shows the breaking apart of the cell membrane?

   Step 4 matches diagram E.

5. *Think!*

   • Diagram A is the last choice. It shows two new identical cells.

   Step 5 matches diagram A.

2
Breakthrough
How Materials Enter and Exit a Cell

What You Need to Know

Materials enter and leave cells through the cell membrane. The amount of any one kind of substance within a cell generally remains fairly constant, but the same particles of each substance do not stay in the cell forever. Small amounts of each substance are constantly leaving and being replaced by the same amounts of new identical material entering the cell.

Not all materials can pass through the cell membrane. What gets through depends on the size of the material and of the openings in the membrane. The movement of materials through a cell's membrane is regulated by other factors, such as pressure. The materials move toward the side of the membrane with the least pressure. The passage of water and dissolved materials through the cell membrane, caused by differences in pressure on the two sides of the membrane, is called **filtration**.

Similarly, the pumping action of your heart creates pressure that pushes blood along pathways in your body called **blood vessels**. Large blood vessels called **arteries** carry blood away from the heart. **Veins** are also large blood vessels, but they carry blood back to the heart. These larger blood vessels are connected to each other by smaller blood vessels, called **capillaries**. Capillary walls are so thin that they are like cell membranes. Greater pressure inside a capillary tends to push materials out of the blood vessel, just as greater pressure inside a cell tends to push materials out of the cell. Thus, while

capillaries are not cells, they can be used to illustrate how materials filter through cell membranes.

Cells are made mostly of water. Water either leaves or enters a cell, depending on the number of water **molecules** (smallest particles of a substance) on the inside and outside of the cell membrane. All molecules are in constant motion. Thus, the water molecules inside and outside a cell are constantly striking against the cell membrane. There is more movement from the side of the membrane that has more water molecules to the side that has less. This is because when the number of water molecules hitting against the cell membrane is large, it is more likely that one of them will hit and pass through an opening in the membrane. This movement of water through a cell membrane is called **osmosis**.

Exercises

1. A **solution** is a mixture of water and dissolved particles of a substance. Match the diagrams with the following descriptions of different kinds of solutions within a cell.

   a. A **concentrated solution**, containing a small number of water molecules and a large number of dissolved particles.

   b. A **dilute solution**, containing a large number of water molecules and a small number of dissolved particles.

Legend:
H_2O – water molecule
DP – Dissolved Particle

A

B

CELL'S OUTSIDE SURFACE

CELL'S INSIDE SURFACE

2. The diagram on page 16 shows enlargements of the out-side and inside surface of a cell membrane, represented by a trampoline with a hole in the center. The cartoon char-acters of water molecules and dissolved particles bounc-ing on the trampoline represent the way these substances strike against a cell membrane. Read the following state-ments, then decide whether they are true or false in de-scribing the diagram.

   a. There are more water molecules hitting against the outside than the inside of the cell membrane.

   b. Water will tend to move out of the cell.

   c. The number of dissolved particles inside the cell helps to prevent the water from leaving the cell.

Activity: PASSING THROUGH

Purpose To symbolize how size affects movement of par-ticles through a cell membrane.

Materials ½ cup (125 ml) table salt
½ cup (125 ml) pinto beans
quart (liter) jar with lid
colander
large bowl
helper

Procedure

1. Pour the salt and beans into the jar.

2. Secure the lid and shake the jar back and forth several times to thoroughly mix the salt and beans.

3. Hold the colander over the bowl as your helper opens the jar and pours its contents into the colander.

4. Gently shake the colander up and down several times.

5. Observe the contents of the colander and bowl.

Results The salt falls through the holes in the colander and into the bowl. The beans remain in the colander.

Why? Cell membranes act like the colander, allowing passage of only those particles small enough to pass through the holes (in this case, salt). Particles larger than the holes (pinto beans) are prevented from passing through. A cell membrane that has holes large enough to admit water but too small to admit many larger particles is called a **semipermeable membrane**. This type of membrane allows only certain sized particles to pass through it.

Solutions to Exercises

1a. *Think!*

- Which diagram has fewer water molecules and more dissolved particles?

Figure B is a concentrated solution.

b. *Think!*

- Which diagram has more water molecules and fewer dissolved particles?

Figure A is a dilute solution.

2a. *Think!*

- The enlarged area of the outside surface of the cell has three times as many water molecules.

Statement A is true.

b. *Think!*

- Water moves through a cell membrane from the side with the most water molecules.

- Most water molecules in the diagram are on the outside, not the inside, of the cell membrane.

Statement B is false.

c. **Think!**

- The dissolved particles in the concentrated solution inside the cell take up space on the membrane and thus restricting the water molecules from striking and leaving through the cell membrane in that area.

Statement C is true.

3
Brainpower

Parts of the Brain and Their Jobs

What You Need to Know

The brain is the control center of your body. It acts like a computer as it sorts input information and gives output instructions about how the body is to behave. The size of the brain changes from about 14 ounces (397 g) at birth to about 46 ounces (1,305 g) in adulthood.

The brain is not one mass but is divided into parts. One of the smaller, less obvious parts is the **hypothalamus**. The hypothalamus regulates automatic body functions, such as pulse rate. For more information about the hypothalamus, see chapter 6.

The three main parts of the brain are the **medulla**, the **cerebellum**, and the **cerebrum**. The medulla and cerebellum are located at the base of the cerebrum. The medulla is connected to the top of the large bundle of nerves running down through the spine, called the **spinal cord**. The medulla controls **involuntary movements** (body movements that happen without your controlling them), such as the beating of your heart. For more information about the medulla, see chapter 4.

The cerebellum, which means "little brain," is a small pear-shaped section at the base of the cerebrum. It controls your **voluntary movements** (body movements that you can control), such as raising your arm. Your cerebellum makes the muscles in your hands and fingers work together smoothly. The cerebellum also helps you keep your balance as you walk,

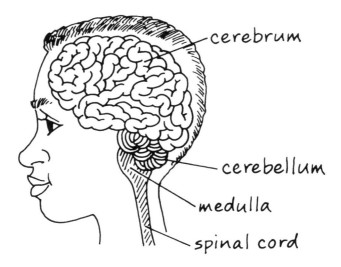

run, or stand. You would have poor balance and move with jerky motions if this part of your brain were injured. See chapter 5 for more information about the cerebellum.

The cerebrum is the largest and most complex part of the brain. It enables you to think, remember, make decisions, and imagine. The cerebrum also makes it possible for you to see, hear, taste, touch, and smell. Even with perfect eyes, you could not see if the messages did not reach the cerebrum.

The cerebrum has two halves, known as the left and right hemispheres, which are covered with a layer of nerve cells called the **cortex**. The right side of the cortex controls muscle activities in the left side of the body, and the left side of the cortex controls activities in the right side of the body. If you are right-brain, you think more with the left side of your cortex, which controls your speech, reading, writing, and math skills. The right side, which controls your emotions and creative expression is used more if you are left-brain.

The cortex has a folded surface, so it looks like an oversized, wrinkled walnut. The folds make it possible for the cortex's large surface area to fit into the small space of the skull. The

development of the cerebrum and the folded cortex is what gives you and other humans more intelligence than other animals.

Exercises

1. Some things can be memorized more easily than others. Look at each of the following lists for one minute. Make an effort to memorize each list. Which list is easier to memorize?

List A	List B
OIZ	ABC
BXQ	DEF
RUL	GHI
QXY	JKL
GZC	MNO

2. Ways of organizing material to help you remember it quickly and easily are called **mnemonic devices**. This method of learning relates the material to be learned to something that's easier to remember, such as a word or phrase. For example, the order of the colors of the spectrum—red, orange, yellow, green, blue, indigo, violet—can be remembered more easily if you use their first letters to form the name "Roy G. Biv."

The parts of a living organism, listed below, are in order from the smallest part to the largest. Design a mnemonic sentence to aid in memorizing the words in order.

Atoms, Molecules, Cells, Tissues, Organs, Systems, Organism

Activity: CONCENTRATION

Purpose   To test your power of concentration.

Materials chair

Procedure

1. Sit in a chair with your feet on the floor.

2. Use your right foot to trace a clockwise pattern on the floor.

3. Keep your foot going in a circle while you move your right hand around in a clockwise pattern in front of your body.

4. Continue tracing the circular pattern with your foot, but change the hand pattern to an up-and-down motion.

Results   It is easy for the foot and hand to perform the same pattern of movement, but difficult to move them simultaneously in two different patterns.

Why?   When the patterns for hand and foot are the same, repetitive movement is easy. Up-and-down or circular patterns are easily done, but only when one pattern at a time is being processed by the brain. It takes much concentration and practice to successfully accomplish both patterns simultaneously.

Solutions to Exercises

1. *Think!*

- Both lists A and B are nonsense syllables, making it necessary to memorize each letter in the list.

- Is there a pattern that makes one list easier to learn? Yes, list B is in alphabetical order.

List B is easier to memorize.

2. *Think!*

- There are many possible answers. All that matters is that you be able to remember the one you chose. Here's one of my favorites:

Another Man Called To Order Some Oysters.

4
Controller

How Your Body Functions without Your Directing It

What You Need to Know

Involuntary movements are made by your body without your having to think about doing them, such as breathing, blinking, sneezing, swallowing, and the beating of your heart. The part of the brain that controls these and other involuntary actions is the medulla.

The outside of the medulla looks like a swollen lump at the top of the spinal cord, but inside are two large cords of nerve fibers, one from the right and one from the left hemisphere of the cerebrum. The cords cross; thus, the left hemisphere of the brain controls muscle movement in the right side of the body and the right hemisphere controls movement in the left side of the body.

Inside the medulla are cells that are very sensitive to the amount of a gas called carbon dioxide that is in the blood. When the carbon dioxide level in the blood increases due to events such as exercising, these special cells send messages that increase the rate and depth of **breathing** (the mechanical process of moving air into and out of the body). You breathe more slowly and less deeply when you are sitting and reading a book than after playing a game of basketball. Your medulla controls this change.

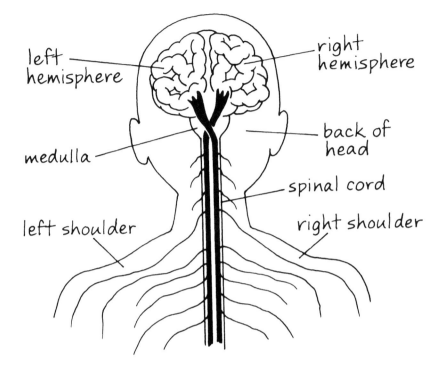

You can control the rate and depth of breathing, but only to a limited degree. You can hold your breath for only a short period of time, because your body gets rid of carbon dioxide every time you **exhale** (breathe out, expelling gases from the lungs). Holding your breath causes the amount of carbon dioxide in your blood to increase. Eventually, when the amount of carbon dioxide reaches a certain point, the medulla overrides your control and you have to breathe. See chapter 17 for more information about your breathing mechanisms.

Exercises

1. Study the graph showing the carbon dioxide level for different activities. Determine which activity causes the carbon-sensitive cells in the medulla to be:

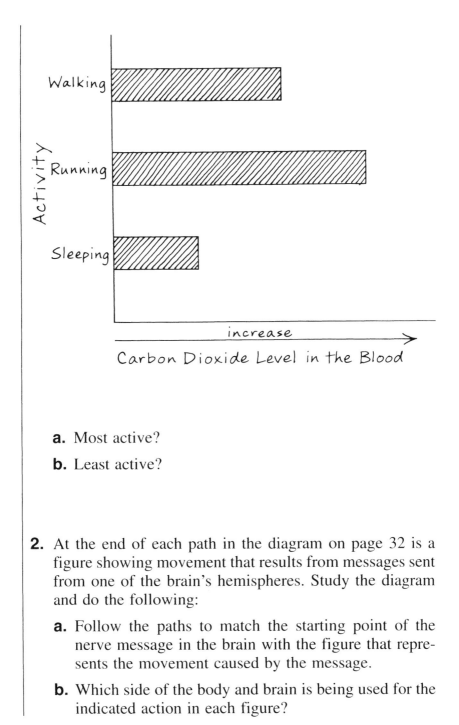

a. Most active?

b. Least active?

2. At the end of each path in the diagram on page 32 is a figure showing movement that results from messages sent from one of the brain's hemispheres. Study the diagram and do the following:

a. Follow the paths to match the starting point of the nerve message in the brain with the figure that represents the movement caused by the message.

b. Which side of the body and brain is being used for the indicated action in each figure?

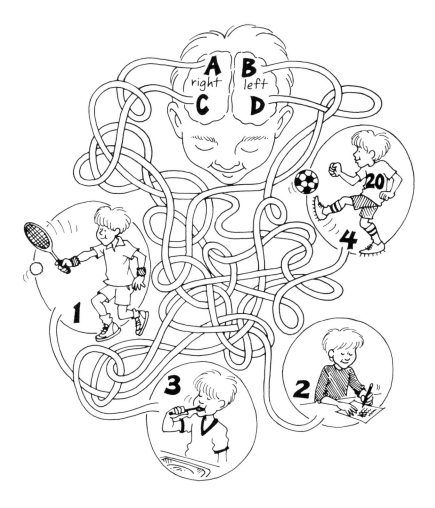

Activity: BACKWARD

Purpose   To test your ability to control movements on different sides of your body.

Materials   helper

Procedure

1. Extend your arms in front of your body and clasp your hands together.

2. Ask your helper to point at but not touch one of your fingers.

3. You must immediately lift the identified finger without lifting any of your other fingers.

4. Observe how quickly you can move the identified finger.

5. Repeat steps 2 through 4 at least four times.

6. Repeat the procedure, but this time cross your arms before you extend them. Then, clasp your hands together and bring them up and close to, but not touching, your chest.

Results   You can easily raise the identified finger when your hands are clasped in the first position, but it is difficult to lift the correct finger when your arms are crossed.

Why?   Your eyes see your fingers and determine which ones are on the right and which are on the left. To move your right index finger, a message must be sent along a nerve cord starting in the left side of your brain. This nerve cord moves through the medulla, where the nerve cord crosses to the right and continues down the right side of your spinal cord. Messages from this nerve cord are sent to the muscles in the finger, causing it to move. It is difficult to instantly move the fingers when your arms are crossed, because you cannot quickly identify the fingers as being on the left or right hand. When your arms are crossed, your left hand is where your right hand should be and your right hand is where your left hand should be.

Solutions to Exercises

1a. _Think!_

- A high amount of carbon dioxide in the blood causes the carbon-dioxide sensitive cells in the medulla to work harder.

- Which exercise on the graph causes the highest level of carbon dioxide in the blood?

Running would cause the carbon-sensitive cells in the medulla to be most active.

b. _Think!_

- Which exercise on the graph causes the lowest level of carbon dioxide in the blood?

Sleeping would cause the carbon-sensitive cells to be least active.

2a. _Think!_

- The messages from the right side of the brain control muscle movements on the left side of the body, and messages from the left side of the brain control muscle movements on the right side of the body.

- Where does each nerve path lead?

Path A: Figure 2
Path B: Figure 3
Path C: Figure 4
Path D: Figure 1

b. *Think!*

- Which side of the body and brain is being used in each figure?

Figure 1: Right arm and hand, left brain
Figure 2: Left hand, right brain
Figure 3: Right arm and hand, left brain
Figure 4: Left leg and foot, right brain

5
Balancing Act

How Your Body Maintains Its Balance

What You Need to Know

The cerebellum is about the size of a pear and is located below and to the rear of the cerebrum. One of the duties of the cerebellum is to coordinate your movements when the cere-

brum gives the command. This is important for such activities as walking, running, writing, or playing ball. When you throw a ball, the decision to throw the ball and the direction in which to throw it comes from the cerebrum. Then, the cerebellum receives messages from body parts such as ears, eyes, and muscles. It uses all this information to coordinate the movements of your fingers, hand, and arm so that their motion is smooth and accurate.

Another duty of the cerebellum is to help you maintain your sense of balance. The body stays balanced as long as its **center of gravity** (point at which an object balances) does not extend past its foundation (the feet). The cerebellum orders and processes split-second actions that require no thought. If you slip on a banana peel while walking, your body starts to fall backward because your center of gravity changes. A message of this movement is sent to the cerebellum, which in turn sends messages to the correct muscles. The muscles respond properly by shifting your body in the opposite direction—forward—so that you regain your balance. Imagine having to ask yourself, Which muscles should I contract? Which muscles should I relax? Where should my arms and hands be held? If these decisions were not made fast enough, you would fall and possibly injure yourself. But because the cerebellum can make speedy decisions, the right messages are sent to each muscle and you regain your balance.

Exercise

A tightrope walker lifts his leg to the side. Which diagram on the next page shows the position that will most likely result in keeping his body balanced so that he does not fall?

A

B

C

Activity: IN THE WAY

Purpose   To demonstrate the body's automatic balance responses.

Materials   wall

Procedure

1. Stand away from the wall with your feet about 12 inches (30 cm) apart and your arms held to your sides.

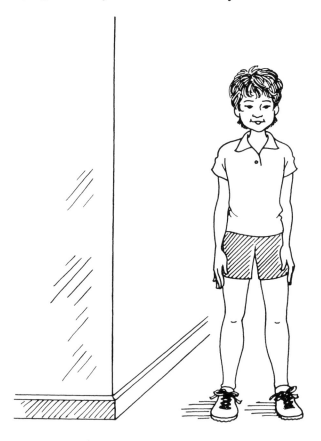

2. Bend your left knee so that your left foot is lifted about 4 inches (10 cm) above the floor.

3. Return your foot to the floor and move next to the wall.

4. Stand as before with your feet about 12 inches (30 cm) apart and with your right foot and right shoulder against the wall.

5. Again, bend your left knee so that your left foot is lifted about 4 inches (10 cm) above the floor.

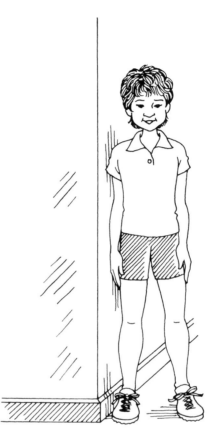

Results   You can bend your knee and raise your foot without being off balance when you are not standing next to the wall. When standing next to the wall, you will fall over if you raise your foot.

Why?   Raising the left foot causes the body's center of gravity to extend past the body's supportive foundation—the foot on the floor. The body automatically leans slightly to the right to redistribute the body's weight and again place its center of gravity over the supportive foot. When standing next to the wall, the body is prevented from leaning to the right, so you cannot balance at all with your foot raised.

Signals to lift the foot are sent by the cerebrum to the cerebellum. As the body action is carried out, other signals from the body are sent to the cerebellum. The cerebellum compares all this information. If a movement would cause the body to be off balance, the cerebellum sends signals to the cerebrum, which then sends appropriate corrective signals to the muscles. Thus, the foot is used to keep your body balanced. You can concentrate and lift your foot, but it will quickly return to its original position to prevent your body from falling.

Solution to Exercise

Think!

- Lifting the leg causes the body's center of gravity to shift past its supportive foundation—the foot on the tightrope.

- How can this shift be corrected? By leaning in a direction opposite that of the raised leg.

Figure C shows the position that will result in keeping the tightrope walker balanced.

6
Regulator

How Your Body Monitors Its Temperature

What You Need to Know

Animals that are able to maintain a constant internal body temperature, even when the temperature outside their bodies changes, are called **endotherms**. These animals are sometimes called warm-blooded animals. Humans are endotherms. The average internal body temperature of humans is about 98.6 degrees Fahrenheit (37° Celsius), but it increases or decreases slightly throughout the day. Body temperatures above 100°F (37.8°C) or below 97°F (36.1°C) are considered abnormal.

The regulation of the inner body temperature of all warm-blooded animals depends on the production of heat by chemical reactions within the body and its distribution by the blood. When the environment is cold, the body must conserve heat to prevent **hypothermia** (excessively low body temperature). In a hot environment, the body must release heat to prevent **hyperthermia** (excessively high body temperature).

The human body has receptors that detect internal changes in the body's temperature. The hypothalamus monitors the temperature of the blood. It is this internal thermostat that enables you to maintain a constant body temperature during periods of exercise or high environmental temperatures. When the temperature of the blood begins to rise, heat sensors in the **anterior** (front) portion of the hypothalamus detect the change.

The hypothalamus sends commands that start activities by which the body cools itself. One cooling action is the **dilation** (expansion or enlargement) of blood vessels near the skin and the **constriction** (contraction or reduction) of blood vessels deeper in the body. This brings warm blood close to the skin's surface, which gives the skin, especially on your face, a reddish appearance. Heat in the blood carried by the dilated blood vessels near the skin is lost to the air. For more information about how the body regulates its temperature, see chapter 8.

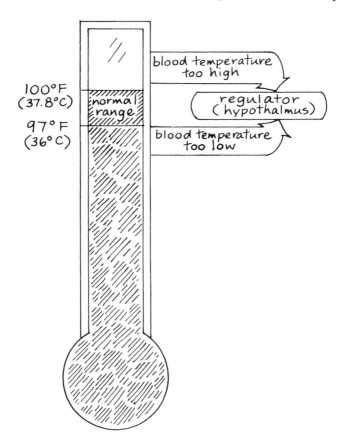

The receptors in the **posterior** (rear) part of the hypothalamus detect colder than normal blood. In order to keep heat within the body, the commands sent by the hypothalamus when it senses cold blood result in a more or less opposite chain of events. The surface blood vessels constrict, which moves the blood farther away from the skin's surface. This makes it more difficult for the heat in the blood to be lost. Muscles around the hair **follicles** (depressions beneath the skin from which hair grows) contract, causing tiny bumps on the skin, commonly called **goose bumps**. These contracted muscles make the hairs stand upright, trapping air to help insulate the body.

Shivering, which is a contraction of skeletal muscles, also produces heat. At the command of the hypothalamus, the body increases **metabolism** (all the chemical and physical processes of the body), resulting in an increase in internal heat.

Exercises

1. Which activity would alert the anterior portion of the hypothalamus?

A

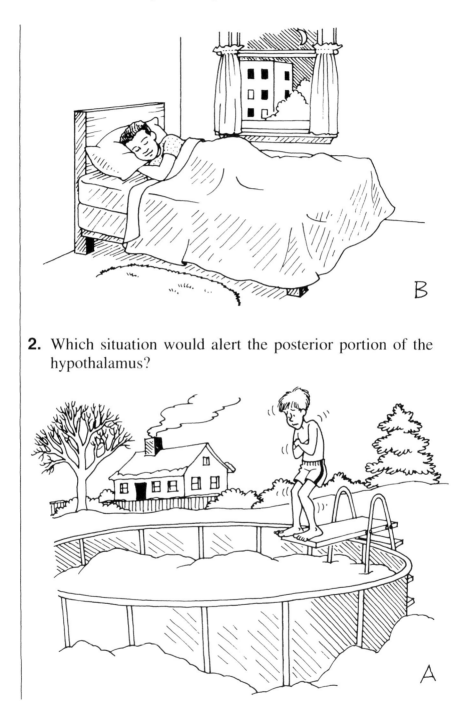

2. Which situation would alert the posterior portion of the hypothalamus?

Activity: HOT OR COLD?

Purpose To demonstrate that sensations of cold or hot can be deceiving.

Materials three 2-quart (2-liter) bowls
cold and warm tap water
5 ice cubes
spoon
thermometer

Procedure

1. Fill two of the bowls three-fourths full with cold tap water.

2. Allow one bowl of water to stand for 5 minutes in order to reach room temperature, which will be called the medium water.

3. Add the ice cubes to the second bowl of water. Stir with a spoon until the ice cubes are about half melted. This will be called the cold water.

4. Fill the third bowl three-fourths full of warm tap water. This will be called the warm water.

5. Use the thermometer to measure the temperature of the warm water. It should be about 113°F (45°C).

   CAUTION: If it is hotter, add cold tap water, stir with a spoon, and check the temperature before proceeding.

6. Place the bowls on a table with the cold water on your right-hand side, the medium water in the middle, and the warm water on your left-hand side.

7. Put your right hand in the cold water and your left hand in the warm water.

cold   medium   warm

8. After 20 seconds, remove your hands from the outer bowls and put both hands in the center bowl of medium water.

Results   The same water feels warm to your right hand but cold to your left hand.

Why?   Heat tends to flow from an object with a higher temperature to an object with a lower temperature. When heat energy is drawn away from the skin, heat sensors respond with a message that the object being touched feels cold. When heat energy is received by the skin, the message is that the object feels warm or hot. The medium water feels warm to your right hand because it had been soaking in icy water. The heat energy flowed from the warm water to your skin. The skin of your left hand was warmer than the medium water. Thus, the energy flow was away from the skin, making the medium water feel cold to this hand.

Solutions to Exercises

1. *Think!*

   • What blood temperature changes does the anterior part of the hypothalamus detect? Above normal temperatures.

   • Which activity would tend to raise the blood temperature?

   The activity in diagram A would alert the anterior portion of the hypothalamus.

2. *Think!*

   • What blood temperature changes does the posterior part of the hypothalamus detect? Below normal temperatures.

- Which situation would tend to lower the body's temperature?

The situation in diagram A would alert the posterior portion of the hypothalamus.

7
Quick Action

How Your Body Automatically Responds to a Stimulus

What You Need to Know

Your body sends messages to and from your brain and spinal cord through special fibers called **nerves**. Nerves are made of bundles of thousands of nerve cells called **neurons**. Electric signals, called **impulses**, travel from one neuron to another. These tiny electrical charges travel in one direction along definite paths. Some impulses travel at speeds of about 250 miles (400 km) per hour. The speed of impulses varies. For example, pain signals are slower than touch signals. If you fall off your bicycle, you feel the pain after you feel the touch.

Impulses are activated by a **stimulus** (something that temporarily excites or quickens a response). Stimuli, in turn, activate **sensory receptors** (cells that receive stimuli of sight, hearing, smell, taste, and touch). Sensory receptors make you aware of your environment. For more information about stimuli and sensory receptors, see chapter 9.

Sensory neurons carry impulses from sensory receptors in areas such as your eyes, nose, and skin to the spinal cord. **Motor neurons** carry impulses to muscles and other parts of the body. Incoming sensory messages are transferred to outgoing motor messages through a relay station called **association neurons**, located in the brain and spinal cord.

The brain controls many of your actions, but sometimes it is necessary for your body to react quickly. When an automatic

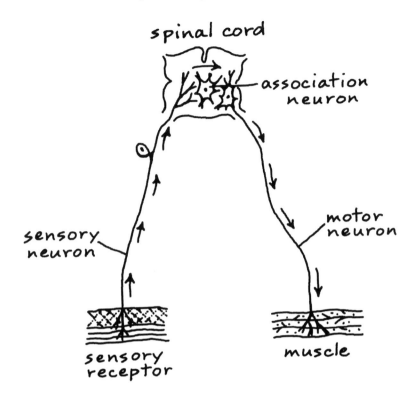

response to a stimulus is made without the brain's direct involvement, the action is called a **reflex**. A reflex is a response that happens so quickly that you do not think about it until after it happens. Reflexes include blinking, coughing, and sneezing. Some reflexes are in response to the threat of physical harm, such as jerking your hand away from a hot object or jumping when frightened.

If you accidently prick your finger with a needle, your hand immediately jerks away. The impulse in this situation bypasses your brain and travels only to and from the spinal cord. First, sensory receptors in your finger receive a message about the needle prick. The sensory neuron in your finger then sends an impulse to the spinal cord, where the signal is sent along two paths. One path is a short reflex loop through the association neurons and back out along the motor neuron to the muscles of the arm and hand. The muscles contract, causing your finger to pull away from the sharp object.

The other path leads up the spinal cord to the brain. When the impulse following this route arrives, you become aware of the pain, but the reflex action has already caused your finger to pull away.

Reflexes that do not depend on previous experience are called **unconditioned reflexes**. You are born with them. Examples include the dilation of the pupils of your eyes when the lights are dimmed and the production of saliva when food enters your mouth.

A **conditioned reflex** is one in which a new stimulus is substituted for the original stimulus. These reflexes partly depend on previous experience. For example, your mouth normally produces excess saliva when the taste buds are stimulated by the chemicals in food that touch them. But if you have eaten something that you really like, the saliva can start to flow just be seeing, smelling, or even thinking about this tasty food. This is a conditioned reflex.

Exercises

1. Match the labels on the diagram on page 56 with the following list of terms:

sensory neuron

association neuron

sensory receptor

motor neuron

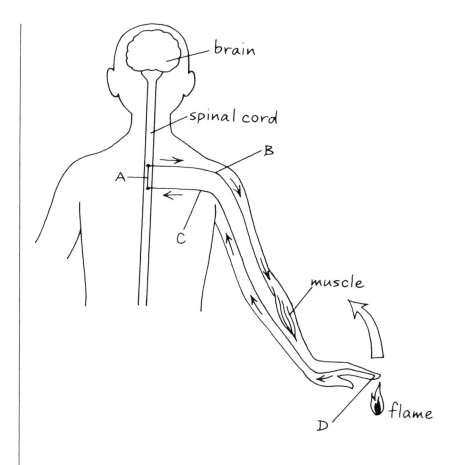

2. Answer the following questions by studying the drawings on the next page. The drawings represent a conditioned reflex that causes the pupil to constrict, or become smaller.

   a. What is the original stimulus?

   b. What is the substituted stimulus?

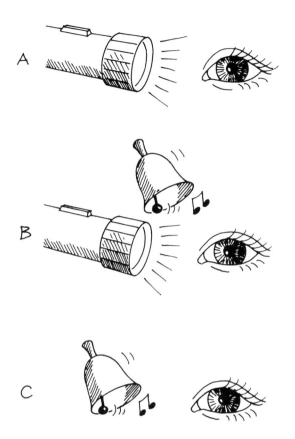

Activity: BLINKING

Purpose To determine if blinking is an involuntary action.

Materials helper who wears glasses or lightly tinted sunglasses
cotton ball

Procedure

*CAUTION: Do not substitute materials without adult approval.
It could be dangerous to throw anything other than a cotton
ball.*

1. Have your helper wear his or her glasses or a pair of sunglasses.

   NOTE: If sunglasses are used, they must be lightly tinted so that you can easily see your helper's eyes through them.

2. Stand about 1 yard (1 meter) away from your helper.

3. Without letting your helper know it's coming, throw a cotton ball directly at your helper's face. The glasses will keep the cotton ball from hitting your helper in the eyes.

Results   Your helper will blink and possibly jerk as well as raise a hand to protect his or her eye.

Why?   The sudden unexpected approach of the cotton ball causes your helper's eyes to blink. Blinking is a reflex action. Like other reflex actions, it is not controlled by thinking about it. The involuntary movement of the eyelids, head, and hand happens because sensory neurons in the eyes send messages to association neurons in the brain and spinal cord. The instructions are then quickly passed on to the muscles, resulting in the protective movements of blinking, jerking the head, and raising the hand in front of the face.

Solutions to Exercises

1. *Think!*

   • Which is the path that carries impulses from the sensory receptors to the spinal cord?

   Part C is the sensory neuron.

   Think!

   • Which is the relay station in the brain and spinal cord that transfers incoming sensory messages to outgoing motor messages?

   Part A is the association neuron.

   Think!

   • Which is the structure that makes you aware of your environment and receives messages about stimuli?

   Part D is a sensory receptor.

   Think!

   • Which is the path that carries impulses from the spine to the muscles?

   Part B is the motor neuron.

2a. *Think!*

- The pupil of the eye first constricts when light enters the eye.

The light is the original stimulus.

b. *Think!*

- Ringing a bell normally would have no effect on the eye. But, if the bell is rung every time the light is shined into the eye and this is repeated again and again, eventually the pupil will constrict when the bell is rung, whether the light is on or not.

The bell is the substituted stimulus.

8
Overcoat

How Your Skin Protects You

What You Need to Know

The skin of an adult covers an area of about 2 square yards (1.7 m^2). On most of your body, the skin varies from about 0.04 inches (0.1 cm) to 0.08 inches (0.2 cm) thick. The extremes of skin thickness are about 0.02 inches (0.05 cm) on your eyelids to approximately 0.24 inches (0.6 cm) on the soles of your feet, where your skin encounters the most wear and tear. Your skin is made up of two main layers. The thin outer layer that you can see is called the **epidermis**. Beneath the epidermis is a thicker layer called the **dermis**.

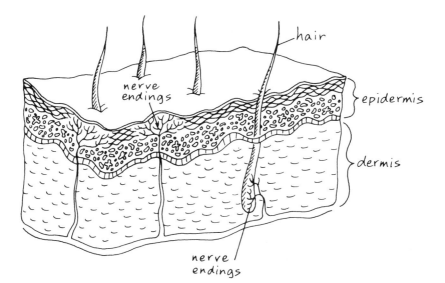

One function of this overcoat called skin is to form a protective barrier against infection, germs, and wear and tear. You live in a world that constantly rubs, scrapes, grinds, cuts, and pushes against your skin. The epidermis is composed of dead cells and **keratin** (a tough protein found in skin, nails, and hair.) These hardened cells overlap to form a tough, almost waterproof covering, but they are easily knocked off when touched. In fact, much of most household dust is made up of dead skin cells. You lose millions of these dead cells every day. In a year's time, as much as 5 pounds (2.3 kg) of dead skin cells can fall off your body.

Your body does not wear away because new skin cells are constantly being made in the dermis. Unlike the epidermis, the dermis is not dead at all. The living cells in the dermis are continually dividing and replacing the dead cells in the epidermis. These new cells push older cells upward. By the time they reach the surface, the old cells are dead and pressed into a flat shape.

The epidermis protects the dermis. The dermis is made of tough elastic cells that give skin its stretchability and springiness. In this layer of skin are the blood vessels that bring nutrients to your skin and the sweat glands and oil glands that keep your skin supple and water repellent. Also in this layer are most of the nerve endings that sense touch, pressure, pain, heat, and cold.

The dermis is not smooth but bumpy. The epidermis fits over these bumps, thus taking on the same pattern. On your fingertips, these patterns are called fingerprints. Each person has a unique fingerprint. These personal signatures develop before birth and never change. Even when the outer skin is damaged, fingerprints remain the same.

All skin contains special cells called **melanin**, which contain grains of brownish black pigment that produce skin color. In the absence of light, the grains cluster together in separate groups, producing skin with a light appearance. In the presence of light, the grains spread out, causing the skin to be darker. Dark skin contains more melanin than light skin. Fair-skinned people can darken their skin by spending time in the sun. A gradual exposure to sunlight promotes the increased production of melanin, commonly called tanning. Melanin helps protect the skin from sunlight. Dark skin is less likely to be damaged by the sun than is fair skin. But overexposure to sunlight of fair and dark skin can cause damage known as sunburn. It is a good idea to cover your skin with protective lotions, such as sunscreen, if you spend a lot of time in the sun. Freckles are caused by uneven distribution of melanin in the epidermis.

Your skin is essential in maintaining a steady internal body temperature of about 98.6°F (37°C). When you get hot, capillaries near the skin dilate and carry more warm blood to the surface, where air touching your skin can cool the blood. This extra blood near the skin is what causes your face to flush when you get hot. Another way your body cools itself is by sweating. When the temperature of the skin increases, sweat glands produce **sweat** (mainly water with salts and other substances dissolved in it). When the sweat absorbs enough heat energy to change to a gas, **evaporation** occurs, taking heat away from your body in the process. For more information on how your body monitors its temperature, see chapter 6.

Skin is covered with a film of natural oil called **sebum** that keeps your skin supple and waterproof. You may have noticed that when you swim for a long time, the skin on your fingers and toes wrinkles. This is because sebum is not made on the fingertips and the skin is not waterproof. When fingers are left under water for a long time, the skin at the tips soaks up water and swells. Because surface skin cells overlap like flat roof tiles, when they absorb water they become too swollen to lay flat and become wrinkled.

Exercise

1. Study the diagrams and determine which represents changes the skin goes through to keep you cooler on a hot summer day.

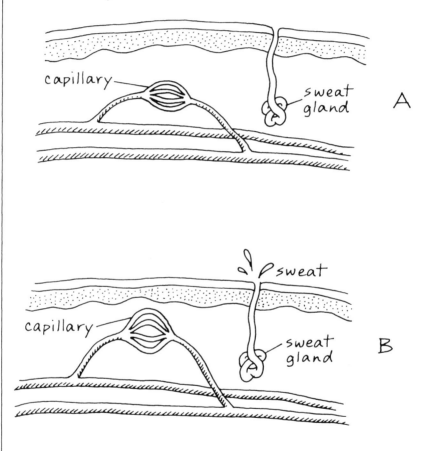

2. If a bandage covers a section of a finger for several days and is then removed, which of the diagrams represents the appearance of the skin covered by the bandage?

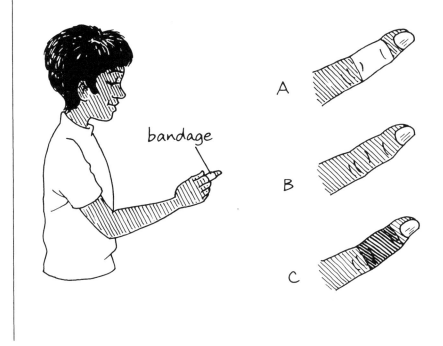

Activity: COOLING OFF

Purpose To show how sweat makes you cooler.

Materials small bowl
tap water
2 thermometers
timer
scissors
paper towel

Procedure

1. Half-fill the bowl with water.

2. Place both thermometers next to the bowl of water on a table. Allow them to sit for 15 minutes.

3. Observe the readings on both thermometers.

4. Cut the paper towel in half.

5. Dip one of the paper towel halves in the bowl of water and place it over the bulb of one thermometer.

6. Place the dry paper towel half over the bulb of the other thermometer.

7. Observe the readings on both thermometers for several minutes.

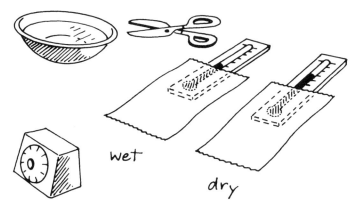

wet

dry

Results The thermometer covered with the wet paper towel has a lower temperature.

Why? The water in the bowl sat long enough to be the same temperature as the air in the room. The wet paper is the same temperature as the dry paper, but the cooling effect is due to evaporation of the water. Evaporation occurs when a liquid absorbs enough heat energy to change to a gas. As the water evaporates, it takes heat energy away from the bulb of the thermometer. The same thing occurs when sweat glands produce sweat that evaporates from the skin. As the sweat evaporates, energy is taken away from the skin, causing the blood near the surface of the skin to cool.

Solutions to Exercises

1. *Think!*

   - When your skin gets hot:

     a. Sweat is produced and evaporates from the skin to cool you.

     b. Blood vessels dilate and get closer to the surface of the skin.

   Diagram B represents changes skin goes through to keep you cooler on a hot summer day.

2. *Think!*

   - The bandage blocks light from the skin.

   - In the absence of light, the grains in melanin cells cluster together in separate groups producing a lighter colored skin.

   Diagram A shows skin that has been covered with a bandage.

9

In Touch

How Sensory Receptors in Skin Keep You in Touch with Your Surroundings

What You Need to Know

When the skin is **stimulated** (excited), different sensations can be felt, such as touch, pressure, heat, cold, and pain. The diagram shows that all sensory receptors in the skin, except pain, are specialized sense organs at the end of nerve fibers. Pain sensors are naked nerve endings.

SENSORY RECEPTORS IN SKIN

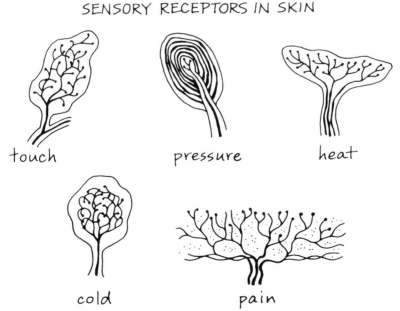

touch   pressure   heat

cold   pain

The distribution of the sensory receptors varies in different parts of the body. Pain fibers form an extensive network and are found in every area. Touch, cold, and heat sensors are located close to the surface of the skin. The face has many heat sensors and is a very temperature-sensitive area. Touch sensors are often found next to a hair follicle. Fingertips have many more touch sensors than an equal area on the wrist, but the wrist has more heat sensors than do fingertips. Because of this, mothers often judge the temperature of milk in a baby's bottle by placing a drop on their wrist. Pressure sensors are found in the underlying tissue of the skin. If the skin is pressed firmly, you experience a sensation of pressure.

The skin can adapt to some sensations to the extent that the feeling lessens or even disappears. The clothes you wear touch your body, but unless they move, you are not constantly aware of their touch. Another example is that water feels warm when you first get into a warm bath but seems to cool quickly. It is not the water that has quickly cooled but your skin's heat sensors that have adapted.

Each sensory receptor is activated by a type of stimulus. The different kinds of sensory receptors and some of the types of stimulus they detect are listed here.

- **Chemoreceptors**—smell and taste
- **Mechanoreceptors**—pressure, touch, and sound
- **Nociceptors**—pain
- **Photoreceptors**—visible light
- **Thermoreceptors**—heat and cold

Exercises

Study each diagram on the next page and determine which sensory receptors are stimulated by the stimulus shown.

Activity: NUMB

Purpose To demonstrate how the brain interprets messages from sensory receptors in the skin.

Materials your hands
pencil

Procedure

1. Use the index finger and thumb of your right hand to rub the upper- and undersides of the index finger of your left hand.

2. Rub back and forth three to four times and make a mental note of this feeling.

3. Hold the pencil in your left hand so that the underside of the index finger on that hand rests against the pencil.

4. Rub your right index finger up and down the upper side of your left index finger, and at the same time rub your right thumb up and down the pencil.

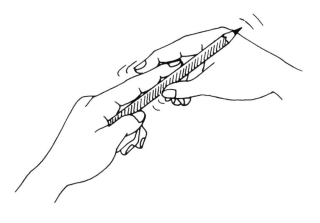

5. Compare the feelings of rubbing the finger with and without the pencil.

Results   When the pencil is held against the finger and both are rubbed, it feels as if part of your finger is numb.

Why?   The brain is like a computer in that it contains certain "programs." When you rub your finger, mechanoreceptors on both sides of the touched finger send messages to the brain. Mechanoreceptors on the finger and thumb of the hand doing the rubbing are also sending messages. These messages are analyzed by the brain, which sends an output message that results in the sensation that you are rubbing both sides of your finger. When the pencil is rubbed instead of the finger's underside, a message is missing. The brain interprets the missing information to mean that the finger is numb on one side. The brain takes in and puts out information based on what the sensory receptors tell it. Even though you know better, the output message is that your finger is numb.

Solutions to Exercises

1. *Think!*

- What is the stimulus? A flower. But the child has her eyes closed, is not touching the flower, and is smiling, which indicates no pain is being felt. Thus, the stimulus is only the smell of the flower.

- Which sensory receptor is stimulated by smell?

The chemoreceptor is stimulated by smell.

2. *Think!*

- What is the stimulus? Music. But the boy does not see the radio behind him. He only hears the sound.

- Which sensory receptor is stimulated by sound?

The mechanoreceptor is stimulated by sound.

3. *Think!*

- The cup is filled with a warm liquid, thus heat is felt. The cup and contents press against the skin of the hands. The child is looking at the cup and smiling (thus no pain is indicated), and the smell of the beverage reaches the nose.

- Which sensory receptors are stimulated by heat, touch, sight, and smell?

Thermoreceptors, mechanoreceptors, photoreceptors, and chemoreceptors are stimulated by heat, touch, sight, and smell, respectively.

10

Hairy, Scratchy Skin

All about Hair and Nails

What You Need to Know

Both hair and nails are types of modified skin. Both develop before a baby is born. In fact, a baby has more hair on its body before it is born than shortly after birth, when the hair on the scalp falls out. A coarser type of hair takes its place, but most of the downy fuzz covering much of the baby's body is retained. Hair is found all over your body, except for a few areas, such as the lips, soles of the feet, and palms of the hands.

All of the hairs on your body grow out of follicles. Only the base of the hair is alive. Cells at the base of each hair are constantly dividing and pushing against each other, causing the cells to become flattened and tightly packed together. As more and more cells accumulate, they are pushed upward through the follicle. These hair cells, like those of the epidermis, are gradually dying as they move farther from their source of nourishment. The hair that you see on your body is made of dead cells and keratin, which give the hair firmness.

Each hair follicle has a blood supply at its base, a tiny erector muscle, and an oil gland. When your skin becomes cold, the erector muscles contract to make your hairs stand up, trapping a layer of air next to the skin. The contracted muscles form

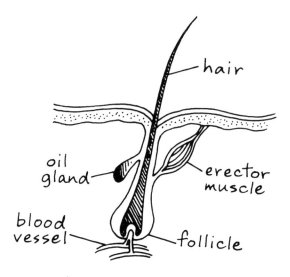

goose bumps. Even though you have fewer hairs than most animals, the hairs still trap air that helps keep you warm. The oil gland produces sebum, which lubricates the hair and skin around it.

The color of your hair, like the color of your skin, depends on how much melanin it contains. Light-colored hair has little melanin, dark-colored hair much more. With age, the center of the hair shaft does not properly develop and tends to become filled with tiny air bubbles. These air bubbles enter the hair only at the base of the hair follicle, and it takes time for the air-filled part of the hair shaft to reach the surface. Thus, the old tale that hair can turn gray overnight because of some emotional strain is doubtful.

The average head of hair grows at the rate of about ½ inch (1.25 cm) per month. Each individual hair strand on your head usually lasts for three to four years, then stops growing and falls out. The hair follicle rests for several months before producing a new strand of hair. It is estimated that we lose between 10 and 100 strands of hair from our head each day and gain about the same number of new ones. Some hair on your body, including eyelashes and brows, does not get as long as hair on your head because it dies and falls off at the end of about three to four months.

Like your hair, the finger- and toenails contain keratin which makes them tough and hard. They grow from a part of the skin called the **nail root**. The thick skin around the edges of the nail is called the **cuticle**. Also like your hair, the cells that make up your nails are dead. That is why you feel no pain when you clip your nails.

Fingernails grow an average of 0.02 inches (0.05 cm) a week, much faster than toenails. Fingernails and hair both grow faster in summer than in winter. Middle fingernails generally grow the fastest. Nails look mostly pink because of the blood vessels in the skin underneath. The half-moon shape at the base of the nail, called the **luna**, is whiter because this area is not firmly attached to the skin. The luna is where all the growth of the nail takes place.

One function of fingernails is to support your fingertips as you touch and handle different objects. Your fingertips would give and flex too much without this rigid support.

Exercises

1. Study the diagram of the child on page 78 and determine which of the areas A through I are not covered with hair.

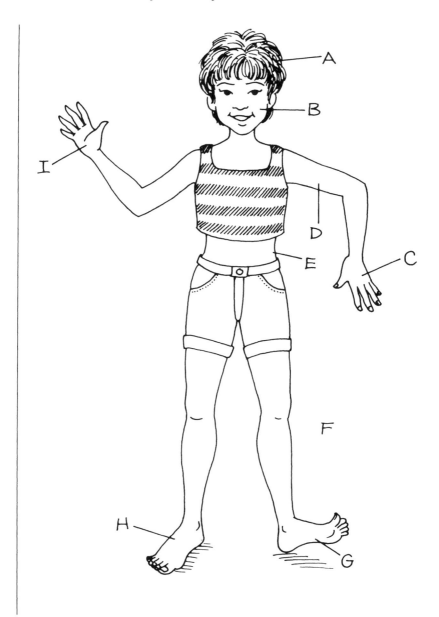

2. Which diagram, A or B, shows the erector muscle contracted so that a goose bump is formed on the surface of the skin?

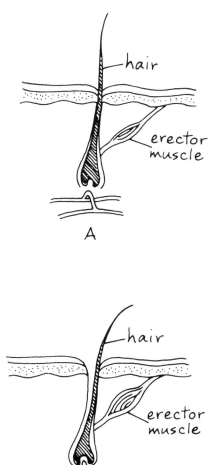

3. Which diagram, A or B, shows the correct location of the luna?

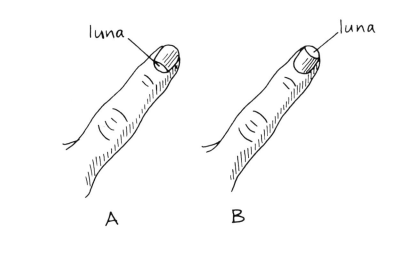

Activity: STRONGER

Purpose To determine which is stronger, straight or curly hair.

Materials 2 strands of hair, one curly (must be naturally curly hair) and one straight
4 paper clips
duct tape
two 3-ounce (90-ml) paper cups
towel
50 pennies

Procedure

1. Ask for a strand of hair about 6 inches (15 cm) long from two different people, one with curly hair and one with straight hair.

2. Prepare a testing instrument with each hair strand by following these steps:

- Thread about ½ inch (1.25 cm) of each end of the hair strand through a paper clip, as shown.

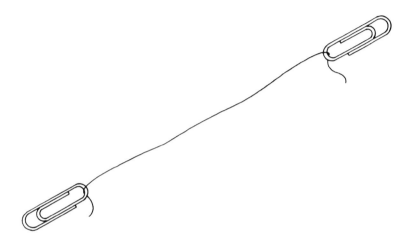

- Use duct tape to secure the loose ends of the hair to the section of hair between the paper clips.

- Tape one of the paper clips to the table edge so that the second paper clip hangs down from the table.

- Open the hanging paper clip to form a hook.

- Insert the paper clip hook onto the side of the paper cup just below the top rim of the cup.

3. Place a towel below the paper cups.

NOTE: The towel will prevent the coins from scattering in the next step.

4. Add the pennies to each hanging cup, alternating one at a time, until one of the hair strands breaks and the cup and coins fall. Make note of the number of coins added to the cup that falls.

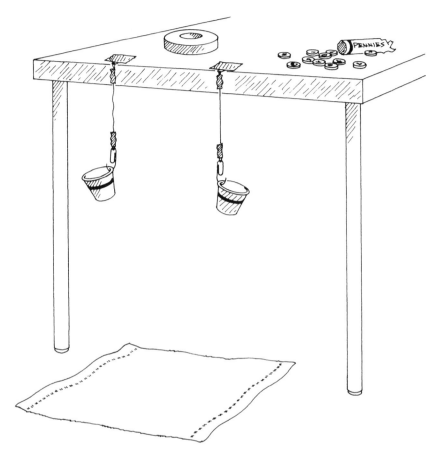

5. Remove the fallen coins and continue adding coins to the remaining cup until the other strand of hair breaks.

6. Compare the number of coins that are required to break each strand of hair.

Results   The exact number of coins needed to break the hair strands will vary, but straight hair usually is stronger.

Why?   The type of hair you have depends partly on the shape of your hair follicles. Curly hair grows from flat follicles, and straight hair from round follicles. The round shape of the straight hair makes it stronger than the flat curly hair.

A type of hair that is neither straight nor curly is called wavy hair, and it grows from oval follicles. Would wavy hair with its slightly rounded shape be stronger than flat curly hair? Discover this for yourself by repeating the experiment using wavy hair.

Solutions to Exercises

1. *Think!*

   • Which areas of the body do not have hair? Lips, soles of feet, and palms of hands.

   Areas G and I are not covered with hair.

2. *Think!*

   • Goose bumps are formed when the erector muscle contracts, causing the hair to stand upright.

   Diagram A shows the erector muscle contracted.

3. *Think!*

   • The luna is shaped like a half-moon and located at the base of the nail.

   Diagram A shows the correct location of the luna.

11
Seeing Is Believing
How Your Eyes Work

What You Need to Know

You interact with the world around you through your five basic senses: sight, taste, hearing, smell, and touch. You enjoy your world more because of your ability to see the colors of a beautiful sunset, taste ice cream, hear a bird sing, smell a flower, and touch the soft fur of your pet. Of these five senses, your eyesight is considered the most important. Almost everything that you remember, from a fun science experiment to the color of your best friend's eyes, is something you have seen.

Your eyes are slightly smaller than a golf ball and are filled with a jellylike fluid. The walls of the eyeball are made of three layers. The inside layer, called the **retina**, is actually the expanded end of the **optic nerve** (main nerve connecting the eye to the brain). This layer contains light-sensitive cells, called **rods** and **cones**, which send messages to the brain. There are about 120 million rods, which detect black-and-white images and work well in dim light. The 6 million to 7 million cones detect color images and do not work well in dim light.

Cones are scattered throughout the retina but are especially abundant in a small, light-sensitive depression, a spot called the **fovea**. The eye's **lens** focuses light on the fovea, the point where objects are clearly seen. At night you mostly see shades of gray, because only your rods are working in the dim light. If your cones are working properly, you are able to detect thousands of different shades of color. People who are not able to see colors are said to be color blind.

Where the optic nerve enters the eye, there are no rods or cones. This spot, the **blind spot**, is insensitive to light. Since your two eyes see things from slightly different angles, each eye compensates for the blind spot of the other. The brain also fills in the missing part of an image so that you do not realize that anything is missing. Find your left eye's blind spot by holding this book at arm's length, facing the page with the dot and X mark. Close your right eye and look at the X in the diagram with your left eye. You must keep facing forward and looking directly at the X. Do not sneak any peeks at the dot. Very slowly, move the book toward your face. When the dot is no longer visible, its image is being focused on your left eye's blind spot. The book will be about 12 inches (30 cm) from your face when the dot disappears.

●   **X**

The second, or middle layer of the eye, called the **choroid**, brings nourishment and oxygen to the eye and contains pigment that gives the eye color. In the front of the eye is a visible colored muscular curtain called the **iris**. In the center of the iris is the **pupil**, a black dot that is actually an opening through which light enters. The size of the pupil is changed by the muscles of the iris. In dim light, the pupil dilates. In bright light, it constricts.

Behind the pupil is the lens, supported by fluid in front and clear jelly behind. The lens is held in place by muscles attached to the choroid. Contraction of these muscles changes the shape of the lens. You see things because light bounces off objects and enters your eyes. The lens focuses the light rays onto the rods and cones on the fovea.

As the light enters the lens, it is **refracted** (bent). The light bends so much that the image appears upside down on the fovea. However, nerve impulses of the image in this position are sent to the brain, where the upside-down image is interpreted as being right side up. If the eyeball is too long, the image is focused in front of the fovea. Nearsighted people have long eyeballs, so images are focused in front of the fovea. They can see things up close but have problems seeing distant objects. Nearsightedness can be corrected by wearing glasses that bend light outward, causing it to focus at a greater distance. Lenses that bend light outward are called **diverging lenses**.

If the eyeball is too short, as it is with farsighted people, the image is focused behind the fovea. Farsighted people can see things at a distance but cannot see close things clearly. **Converging lenses**, which bend the light inward so that it focuses at a shorter distance, are used to correct farsightedness.

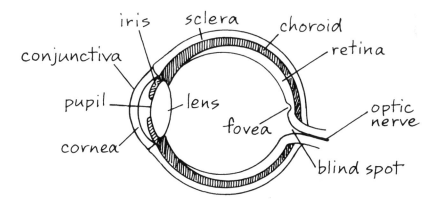

The third, or outer, layer of the eye is a tough covering that forms the "whites" of your eyes. This layer is called the **sclera**. The front of the eye is covered with a bulging, **transparent** (see-through or clear) area of the sclera, called the **cornea**. A thin, transparent film called the **conjunctiva** covers and protects the front of the eye. The conjunctiva is very sensitive to even the smallest particles of dust. Your eyelashes keep specks of dust out of your eyes, and blinking helps to remove dust that gets past the eyelashes. Fluid, called tears, washes the eyes' surface each time the eyelids blink, which is about 15 times a minute.

Exercises

1. Study the diagrams and choose the one that shows how the lens focuses an image onto the fovea.

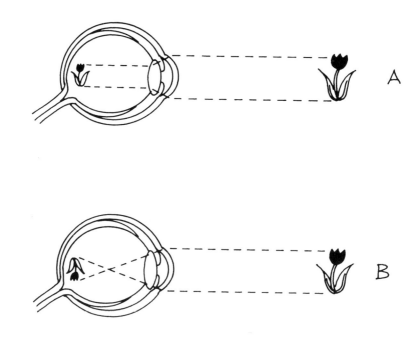

2. The diagrams represent the use of corrective lenses for poor eyesight. Which represents before and after use of corrective lenses for nearsightedness?

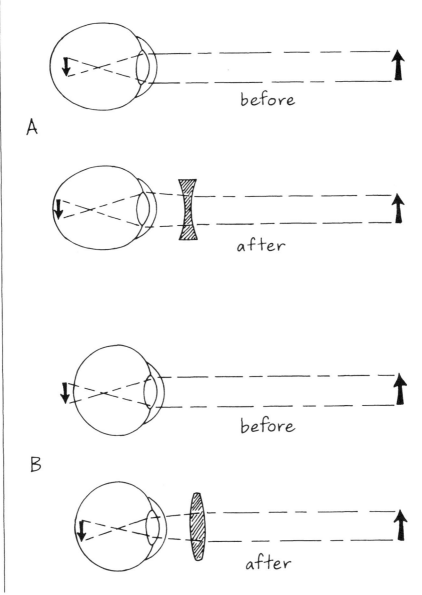

Activity: OPEN AND CLOSE

Purpose To demonstrate the ability of the eye's pupil to change size.

Materials penlight
helper

Procedure

1. Ask your helper to sit in a very dimly lighted room with both eyes open.

2. After 2 to 3 minutes, observe the size of the pupils in both eyes.

3. Hold the penlight close to, but not touching, the side of your helper's face. Slowly move the penlight so that the beam of light moves across the side of the face and shines directly into the pupil of one eye. Immediately turn off the penlight.

   CAUTION: Do not shine the light into your helper's eye for more than 1 second.

4. Repeat the previous step with the opposite eye.

5. Compare the size of the pupils before and after shining the light into the eyes.

Results   The pupils are much larger before shining a light into the eyes.

Why?   The iris controls the amount of light entering the eye by making the opening in its center, the pupil, larger or smaller. In dim light, the pupil dilates, allowing more light to enter the eye. In bright light, the pupil constricts to protect the rods and cones on the back of the eye.

Solutions to Exercises

1. *Think!*

   • The lens turns the images upside down on the fovea.

   • Which diagram shows an upside-down image?

   Diagram B shows how the lens focuses an image onto the fovea.

2. *Think!*

   • Nearsightedness is due to a longer than normal eyeball.

   • If the eyeball is too long, the image is focused in front of the fovea.

   • A diverging lens bends the light outward, causing it to focus at a greater distance.

   Diagram A shows the proper lens used to correct nearsightedness.

12
Sound Effects

How You Make Sounds

What You Need to Know

Speech and other sounds that you use to communicate are produced in your **larynx** (voice box). The larynx is made of muscle tissue and **cartilage** (firm but flexible supportive material), which bulges at the front of the neck. You can feel your bulging larynx by gently rubbing your fingers down the front of your neck. The larynx moves up and down when you swallow. A common name for the larynx is **Adam's apple**. Men generally have a larger, more bulging Adam's apple than women.

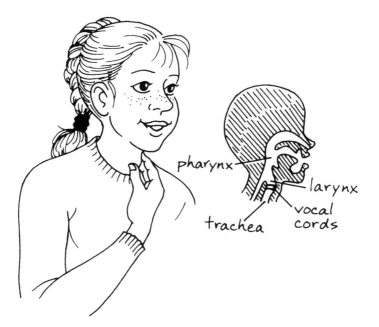

Stretched across the opening of the larynx are two strips of tough, elastic tissue and muscle, called **vocal cords**. Air entering the nose or mouth passes from the **pharynx** (throat) into the larynx, where it must pass between the vocal cords and on to the lungs. The tube through which the air passes is called the windpipe, or **trachea**. Air leaving the lungs takes the reverse path out of the body. Muscles in the larynx move these cords so that they open and close like sliding doors. When the vocal cords are open, as they are when you breathe, they form a triangular shape. When they are pulled closer together, as when you speak, there is a small slit between them. Air passes through this slit, causing the vocal cords to **vibrate** (move to and fro). This vibration produces sound.

The tighter the vocal cords are stretched, the higher the **pitch** (highness or lowness of sound) of the sound produced by their vibration. The size of your vocal cords and larynx also affects the pitch of your voice. Shorter vocal cords produce a higher, pitched voice. Babies' vocal cords are about 0.2 inches (0.5 cm) long. They grow to about 0.8 inches (2 cm) in women and 1.2 inches (3 cm) in men. Most women have higher-pitched voices than men because their vocal cords are shorter.

The loudness of the sound produced is determined by the speed of the air flowing between the vocal cords. The faster the air, the louder the sound. Since more breath is used for shouting, you tend to breathe more deeply and more often when shouting. There is less air moving through the vocal cords when you speak at a normal volume than when you breathe normally. If you speak for long periods of time, you may feel slightly dizzy because the slow airflow during speaking does not bring in enough oxygen to your body.

A cough is an automatic reaction that helps to clear irritating particles out of your breathing passages. The steps leading up to a cough are as follows. First, a deep breath is taken; then the vocal cords close, sealing off the air passage. Air is compressed in the lungs by muscles in the chest and another, large sheetlike muscle between the chest and abdomen, called the **diaphragm**. The vocal cords relax, and air rushes at a high speed out of the lungs, up the trachea, and out the mouth. The speed of the air in some coughs is about 300 miles (480 km) per hour. This fast-moving air causes the vocal cords to vibrate, and thus the coughing sound is made.

Hiccups are caused when your diaphragm contracts and moves down more sharply than usual. Why hiccups begin is not clearly understood. The "hic" sound is due to the vocal cords snapping shut after each short, sudden gasp of breath.

Exercises

1. Study the diagrams of the vocal cords and determine which one shows the position of the vocal cords during the following activities:

   a. normal breathing

   b. singing or speaking

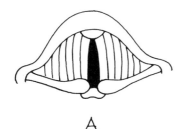 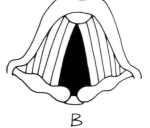

A   B

VOCAL CORDS

2. Study the diagrams and determine which represents a sound produced by slow-moving air through partially closed vocal cords.

Activity: VIBRATING CORDS

Purpose   To determine how you make speech sounds.

Materials hand mirror

Procedure

1. Keep your mouth closed while you hum, making the "mmm" sound of the letter M.

2. While continuing to hum, open your mouth slightly and note the new sound produced.

3. Make the sounds of the following letters, and look in the mirror to observe the shape of your lips and whether your mouth is open or closed. Also note the position of your tongue as you produce each sound:

   D, P, S, A, E, I, O, and U.

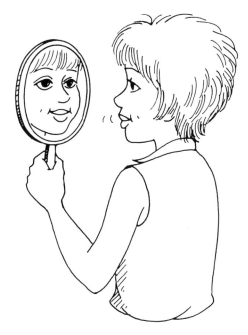

Results The "mmm" sound changes to an "ahh" sound when the mouth is opened. The tongue and lips are in different positions for each of the other letter sounds. Only the humming sound of the letter M requires the mouth to be closed.

Why? Your lips, tongue, cheeks, roof of your mouth, teeth, nasal cavity, and nose help to change, or "shape," the sounds produced by your vibrating vocal cords. The "mmm" sound made with your mouth closed changes to an "ahh" sound because the path of the air flowing out of your head changes when you open your mouth. With your mouth closed, there is little room between your tongue and the roof of your mouth. Opening your mouth moves the tongue down.

The D sound requires that the tongue be placed against the front part of the roof of the mouth, called the **hard palate**. In this position the airflow is blocked. The P sound is also produced by suddenly stopping the flow of air leaving the mouth, but your lips, not your tongue, stop the airflow.

The S sound is made by placing the tongue against the roof of the mouth and forcing air through the narrow opening between the tongue and hard palate.

The shape of your cheeks and lips allow you to form the vowel sounds of A, E, I, O, and U. The shape of your mouth is also changed by moving the lower jaw up and down.

Solutions to Exercises

1a. *Think!*

- During normal breathing, the space between the vocal cords is open.

Diagram B shows the position of the vocal cords during normal breathing.

b. *Think!*

- The vocal cords are drawn together during singing or speaking so that the air passing through will cause them to vibrate.

Diagram A shows the position of the vocal cords during singing or speaking.

2. *Think!*

- The cheerleader is shouting, which produces a loud sound.
- Loud sounds are produced by fast-moving air passing through partially closed vocal cords.
- The child that is whispering is making a low sound.
- Low sounds are produced by slow-moving air passing through partially closed vocal cords.

Diagram B represents a sound produced by slow-moving air through partially closed vocal cords.

13
Smellers

How You Smell Things

What You Need to Know

Smell happens inside your nose. Odors dissolved in the air you breathe pass through your nose and stimulate the tiny chemoreceptors located in the top of the nasal cavity. While there are millions of these cells grouped together, they cover only a small area about the size of a postage stamp. These special cells send a message to the brain, which identifies the smell.

Your sense of smell is about 10,000 times more sensitive than your sense of taste. But, compared to that of other animals, your sense of smell is very poor. Even so, you may be able to recognize thousands of different smells. You never forget a smell. Once your nose has detected the odor of fish, you will always recognize it when you smell it.

The "fishy" smell of fish comes from molecules that leave the fish and enter the air. When air containing these molecules enters your nose, some of the molecules reach the chemoreceptors in your nasal cavity. Each receptor has hairlike bristles covered with a sticky, slippery substance called **mucus**. The "fishy" molecules must first dissolve in this mucus before the bristles start the signal that tells the brain that a fish is nearby.

Scientists do not exactly know how your sense of smell works. It is thought that the molecules of odors have a specific shape that fits into the cells of chemoreceptors, just as a key fits into a lock. This is called the **"lock-and-key" theory**. This might explain why an artificial flavor smells much like the natural flavor. The odor molecules from the artificial and natural sub-

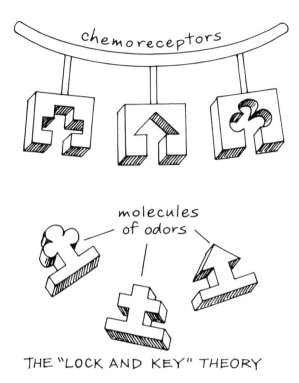

THE "LOCK AND KEY" THEORY

stance may have similar molecular shapes, thus stimulating the same response from the chemoreceptors.

When you have a cold, you often lose your sense of smell because your nose is blocked with excess mucus, preventing scent particles from reaching the chemoreceptors. Your sense of smell can also become **desensitized** (insensitive or nonreactive) to a particular smell if exposed to it for some time. If you enter a house where cabbage has been cooked, you notice the smell immediately. But, after a while, the smell does not seem as strong. This is due to the desensitization of chemoreceptors by constant stimulation with one smell. Once you have become desensitized to a smell, it would have to increase in strength several hundred times before you could smell it as strongly as before. But if you leave the house for a while and return, the smell will again be as strong as when you first entered.

Exercises

Study the diagram and determine which path, A or B, results in the following response:

1. Chemoreceptors on the tongue are stimulated and popcorn is tasted.

2. Chemoreceptors in the top of the nasal cavity are stimulated and popcorn is smelled.

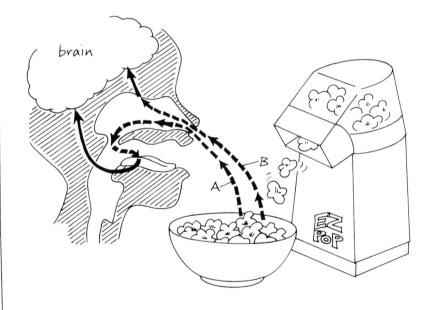

Activity: STRONGER

Purpose To determine how sniffing affects the intensity of smells.

Materials vanilla extract
2 cotton balls
baby food jar
timer

Procedure

1. Place a few drops of the vanilla on one of the cotton balls.

2. Drop the moistened cotton ball into the jar, leaving the lid off.

3. Hold the opening of the jar under, but not touching, your nose.

4. Breathe normally for one or two breaths and note the strength of the smell of the vanilla.

5. Discard the cotton ball.

6. Wait 5 minutes, then repeat steps 1 and 2 with the other cotton ball, again holding the opening of the jar under, but not touching, your nose.

7. Take a good sniff by inhaling deeply.

Result   The smell of the vanilla is stronger when you take a good sniff than when you breathe normally.

Why?   In normal breathing, the air carrying the vanilla molecules passes through the nasal cavity and into the back of the throat. When you take a good sniff, currents of air are drawn upward, flowing over the chemoreceptors located high up at the back of your nose. Sniffing also brings in more air containing the vanilla molecules.

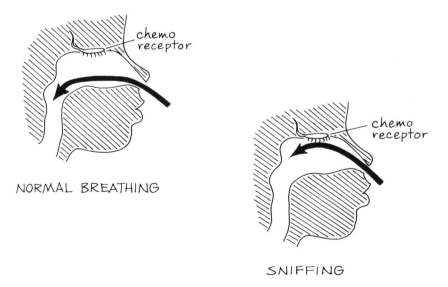

NORMAL BREATHING

SNIFFING

Solutions to Exercises

1. *Think!*

- Odor molecules can drift from the nasal cavity down into the mouth, where they dissolve in the saliva on the tongue and stimulate the chemoreceptors of taste.

- Tastes are experienced when chemoreceptors of taste are stimulated. This is called "tasting a smell."

Path A results in tasting popcorn.

2. *Think!*

- Odor molecules drifting into the nose stimulate chemoreceptors of smell.

Path B results in smelling popcorn.

14
Tasters

How You Taste Things

What You Need to Know

You taste with your tongue. Actually, chemoreceptors called **taste buds** detect the flavor of the foods that you eat. Most taste buds are located on the surface of the tongue, although a few are found on the **soft palate** (back part of the roof of the mouth) and in the throat. A taste bud is made up of receptor cells and support cells clustered together like the wedges of an orange.

To experience taste, chemicals from food must first dissolve in your mouth's **saliva** (liquid that softens and partially digests food). This liquid then moves into the openings at the tops of the taste buds, called **bud pores.** The chemoreceptors, stimulated by the molecules in the dissolved food, send messages to the brain.

Adults can have as many as 10,000 taste buds. The structures that you see on the surface of your tongue are not individual taste buds but as many as 200 taste buds grouped together. These groups are called **papillae.** Four types of taste buds can be distinguished. Each type best detects one of the primary taste sensations: sweet, salt, sour, or bitter. Each of the primary tastes is localized in a special area of the tongue.

Sweet is best tasted at the front of the tongue, salt on the sides of the front near the tip, sour along the side, and bitter at the back of the tongue. All four can be tasted at the back of the mouth and

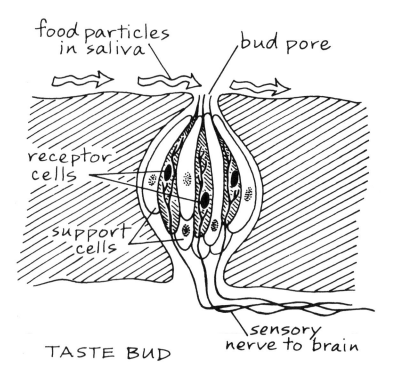

TASTE BUD

in the throat. While there are more of each type of taste bud in specific areas of the tongue, there is considerable overlap of the taste areas and much variation from one person to the next. The flavors of most foods that you eat are a combination of the four tastes of sweet, salt, sour, and bitter.

The tongue is also sensitive to touch, cold, and heat and these sensations affect the sense of taste. Lumpy mashed potatoes seem not to taste the same as smooth ones. Cold foods make your taste buds less sensitive. This is why melted ice cream or warm sodas taste sweeter. The tongue is also sensitive to pain.

Taste is also very dependent on your sense of smell. When you have a cold and your nose is blocked, you find that foods are not as tasty. For more information about the link between the senses of taste and smell, see chapter 13.

Exercises

1. The taste buds are grouped on the diagram of the tongue according to the tastes they detect. Identify each geometric shape as representing the specific taste of sweet, sour, salt, or bitter.

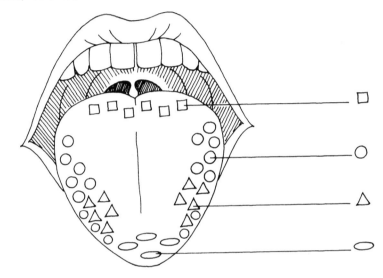

2. Study the diagrams and choose which food, when placed on your tongue, will be the first to stimulate the sweet taste buds.

A   B

Activity: LINKED

Purpose   To determine if smell and taste are linked senses.

Materials   3 different kinds of fruit juice
four 3-ounce (90-ml) paper cups
tap water
scarf that can be used as a blindfold
helper

Procedure

NOTE: Do not let your helper see the juices before the experiment starts.

1. Pour each fruit juice into a cup.

2. Fill the fourth cup with water.

3. Use the scarf to blindfold your helper.

4. Ask your helper to hold his or her nose during the experiment.

5. Hand one cup of juice to your helper and give instructions to drink the juice and identify it.

6. After making the identification, have your helper drink some water to wash out the taste of the juice.

7. Repeat steps 5 and 6 for the other two juices.

8. Repeat the procedure for all three juices without the blindfold and without holding the nose.

Results   When they are not smelled, the juices have a similar taste. When the juices are smelled, their tastes are different and easily recognized.

Why?   When you eat, the taste of the food depends not only on your taste buds but also on the smell of the food. It is the combination of flavor and aroma that makes foods have specific "tastes." When food is in your mouth, it gives off odor molecules, which travel up the connecting passage between the mouth and the nose and enter the nasal cavity. The chemoreceptors at the top of the nasal cavity are stimulated by the odor molecules. It is the combination of the messages sent to the brain by the taste buds and those of the chemoreceptors that allows you to identify the flavors of most foods.

Sometimes it is difficult to know whether you are smelling or tasting a food. Actually, you can "taste" a smell. This happens when odor molecules move from the nose down into the mouth, where they dissolve in the saliva. This mixture stimulates the taste buds on your tongue, and you actually "taste" the air you breathe.

Solutions to Exercises

1a. *Think!*

- The squares are located on the back of the tongue.

- What taste is detected at the back of the tongue?

The square represents bitter.

b. *Think!*

- The circles are located along the sides of the tongue.
- What taste is detected on the sides of the tongue?

The circle represents sour.

c. *Think!*

- The triangles are located on the sides of the front near the tip of the tongue.
- What taste is detected in these areas?

The triangle represents salt.

d. *Think!*

- The ovals are on the tip of the tongue.
- What taste is detected on the tip of the tongue?

The oval represents sweet.

2. *Think!*

- Foods cannot be tasted unless they are dissolved in saliva.
- The solid cube of sugar would have to dissolve in saliva before it could be tasted.
- The liquid honey would mix with the saliva in the mouth, but being a liquid already, it could be tasted sooner.

Honey would be the first to stimulate the sweet taste buds.

15
Receivers

How You Hear Sounds

What You Need to Know

Ears are special organs that are sensitive to sounds. Sounds are produced by the vibrations of objects. When an object vibrates, the vibrations travel through the air in all directions. The outer part of your ear is shaped to receive these vibrations, called **sound waves,** and direct them along a passage, called the **ear canal,** to your eardrum, or **tympanic membrane**.

The eardrum is a thin membrane tightly stretched across the end of the ear canal. Sound waves strike this membrane, causing it to vibrate like the head of a drum. The vibrations from the tympanic membrane are passed on to three tiny bones in the inner ear called, because of their shapes, the hammer, the anvil, and the stirrup. Collectively these three ear bones are called **ossicles**. These bones amplify the sound and span the air-filled gap across your middle ear.

The **eustachian tube** (a narrow tube connecting the middle ear to the throat) ensures that the pressure inside the middle ear is the same as that on the outside of your body. When your ears "pop" on an airplane, in an elevator, or at another high elevation, it's because of the movement of air through the eustachian tube to equalize the pressure inside and outside.

The ossicles carry the vibrations to the inner ear. The hammer is connected to the tympanic membrane, and the stirrup is connected to a membrane called the **oval window,** which covers the entrance to your inner ear. Inside the inner ear is a

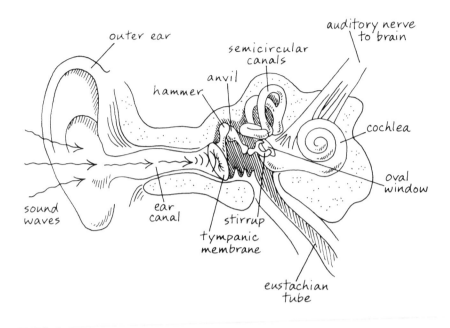

coiled tube called the **cochlea**. The cochlea, which looks much like a snail, is filled with liquid and contains thousands of hairlike mechanoreceptor cells. These sound-sensitive cells pick up the vibrations entering the cochlea, and the **auditory nerve** carries the impulse to the brain, where the sound is identified.

The inner ear also contains three fluid-filled, curved passages, called **semicircular canals**, which are not used for hearing but for maintaining balance. For more information on how the semicircular canals work, see chapter 16.

Exercises

1. The number of sound waves that reach your ear in one second is called the **frequency** of the sound. High-pitched sounds have a greater frequency than low-pitched sounds.

Study the diagram and determine which instrument, A or B, is producing the higher pitch.

NOTE: Each line represents one sound wave.

A   B

2. An animal's or human's ability to hear various frequencies is called its hearing range. Use the graph showing the hearing ranges for different animals to answer questions a through d.

   a. Which animal has the widest range of hearing?

   b. How many animals on the graph can hear higher pitched sounds than you can hear?

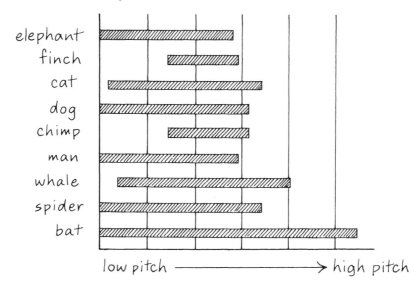

c. Which animal can hear the highest pitched sounds?

d. Can dogs hear sounds that you cannot hear?

3. If you gently tap a table with your finger, you use less energy and produce a quieter sound than if you slap it with your hand. The **intensity** (amount of energy used per second) of a sound compared with the quietest sound the ear can hear is called **noise level**, which is measured in units called **decibels**. Use the graph showing the sounds and noise levels to answer questions a and b.

a. Noise levels above 120 decibels cause pain. Which sounds on the graph cause pain?

b. A noise level above 85 decibels or more can possibly cause damage to your ears. How many sounds on the graph could possibly damage your ears?

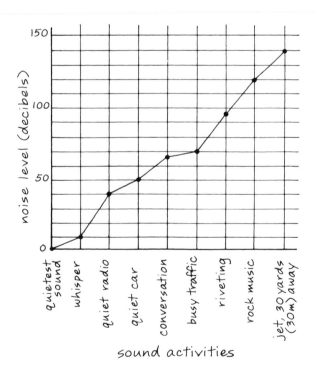

Activity: BIGGER AND BETTER?

Purpose To determine if the size of the outer ear affects hearing.

Materials radio

Procedure

1. Turn the radio on and set it on medium volume.

2. Stand about 1 yard (1 m) in front of the radio.

3. Turn your left ear toward the radio and note the noise level of the sounds from the radio.

4. Turn your back toward the radio and note the noise level of the sounds from the radio.

5. Cup your left hand as shown in the diagram.

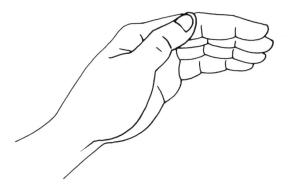

6. Place your cupped hand over your left ear, with your thumb and index finger touching your ear.

7. Again, note the noise level of the sounds from the radio as you stand first with your left ear toward the radio and then with your back toward the radio.

Results   The sounds from the radio are louder with your ear turned toward the radio. The noise level is further increased by placing your cupped hand over your ear.

Why?   Your two outer ears act as sound receivers that funnel sound waves into your ear canal. Placing your hand over your ear and turning the ear toward the radio causes more of the sounds from the radio to be received and directed inside your ear. This is not to say that having a larger outer ear would make you hear all sounds better. In fact, your cupped hand blocks some of the sound waves coming from behind you when your back is toward the radio. If you could move your ears around to "look for" sounds, as do some animals, then a larger ear would help you to receive sounds from different directions.

Solutions to Exercises

1. *Think!*

   • A greater number of sound waves reaching the ear in a given time indicates a sound with a high frequency.

- Sounds with a high frequency have a high pitch.
- Which instrument produces the sound with the higher pitch?

Instrument B, the flute, has the higher pitch.

2a. Think!

- Which animal has the longest bar on the graph?

The bat has the widest range of hearing.

b. Think!

- How many bars on the graph are farther to the right than that for humans?

Six animals can hear higher pitched sounds than you can.

c. Think!

- Which bar extends the farthest to the right?

Bats can hear the highest pitched sounds.

d. Think!

- The bars for dogs and humans start at the same place on the left. Thus, dogs and humans can hear the same low-pitched sounds.
- The bar for dogs extends farther to the right than the bar for humans.

Yes, dogs can hear sounds that you cannot hear.

3a. Think!

- How many points on the graph are above the 120-decibel line? One.

The sound of a jet that is 30 yards (30 m) away can cause pain.

b. *Think!*

- Which sounds have points on the graph above the 85-decibel line? Riveting, rock music, and a jet 30 yards (30 m) away.

Three sounds on the graph can possibly cause damage to your ears.

16
Tilt

How Your Ears Help You Sense Movement

What You Need to Know

Your ears allow you to hear sound, but they also help you to keep your balance. The semicircular canals in your inner ear help to maintain balance. These fluid-filled canals have hair-like mechanoreceptors located at one end of each canal. The canals are at right angles to each other, much like two sides and bottom of a box. The position of the canals allows you to sense movement in three directions: up and down, side to side, and backward and forward.

The movement of your head causes the semicircular canals to move, but the fluid in the canals lags behind and then moves. When you stop, the fluid continues to move for a little while because of **inertia** (the tendency of an object to remain stationary or to continue to move unless acted on by an outside force). The movement of the fluid pushes against the sensory cells, which respond by sending messages of the movement to your brain.

Below the semicircular canals are two tiny sacs, called the **utricle** and **saccule**. Like the semicircular canals, these sacs are involved in detecting motion, but they also determine the position of the head when it is stationary. Both the utricle and the saccule are filled with a fluid, and in their walls are special sensory areas, called **maculae**.

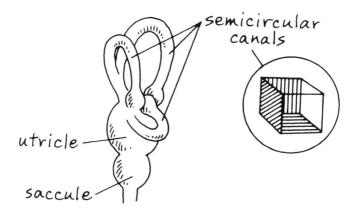

Inside each macula are hairlike sensory cells embedded in a thick jellylike layer containing tiny calcium carbonate crystals, called **otoliths**. The maculae are positioned so that they are almost at right angles to each other, which makes one horizontal when the other is vertical. **Gravity** (the force that pulls everything toward the earth's center) pulls the otoliths downward, stimulating the sensory hairs, which in turn send messages along nerve fibers to the brain. The brain interprets the messages and determines whether you are right side up or upside down. Movement of the otoliths also gives you a feeling of acceleration (speeding up) or deceleration (slowing down).

The inner ear plays a major role in keeping your body balanced, but messages from other body parts, such as your eyes and muscles, are also sent to your brain. By analyzing all these signals, the brain can determine the position of the body and make the proper adjustments to keep you balanced. For more information about balance, see chapter 5.

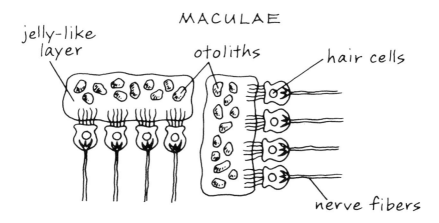

jelly-like layer   MACULAE   otoliths   hair cells   nerve fibers

Exercises

Match the description of each simulated movement of the inner ear with the diagram of a body activity on page 124 that would cause such a movement.

1. A closed jar half filled with water is quickly tilted to one side. The water inside the jar slightly sloshes from side to side for a short time.

2. A glass is half filled with water, the surface of which is covered with black pepper. The glass is turned around on its base eight to ten times. The pepper on the surface continues to spin around for a short time after the glass stops moving, indicating that the water is still moving.

3. A closed jar filled with corn syrup and one marble is turned upside down. The marble gradually moves to the end of the jar that is down.

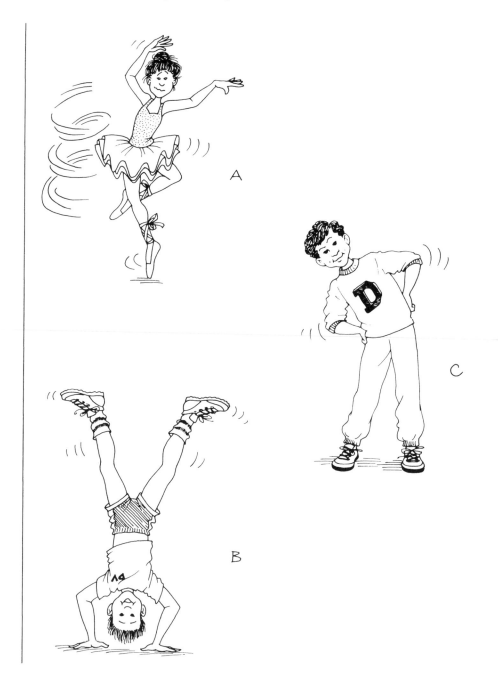

Activity: SPINNER

Purpose   To demonstrate the effect of spinning the body around rapidly.

Materials   swivel chair
          helper

Procedure

1. Position the chair in the center of the floor or any open area.

2. Sit in the chair.

3. Place your hands in your lap and extend your feet outward.

4. Ask your helper to stand behind you with his or her hands on your shoulders.

5. Have your helper start you spinning around and immediately step out of the way.

6. Note how you feel when the chair has stopped spinning.

Results   You will feel dizzy for a short time after you have stopped spinning.

Why?   When you spin around and around, the liquid in the semicircular canals of your ears moves. At first, the fluid resists movement, but as spinning continues the fluid begins to flow in the direction of the spin. When you stop spinning, the fluid resists the stopping motion and sends signals to the brain that you are still spinning.

Solutions to Exercises

1. *Think!*

- The water in the jar, like the fluid in your semicircular canals, does not move with the jar but lags behind.

- Side-to-side movement of your head changes the position of the semicircular canals. The fluid sloshes from side to side in one of the canals as in the tilted jar.

Diagram C represents the body activity that would cause the simulated side-to-side movement of inner ear fluid.

2. *Think!*

- Most of the liquid lags behind when the glass first starts, and then continues to turn after the glass stops, because of inertia.

- Fluid in your semicircular canals has a brief delay in beginning to move but continues to spin after you have stopped.

Diagram A represents the body activity that would cause the simulated spinning of inner ear fluid.

3. *Think!*

- As the jar is inverted, gravity pulls the marble down through the thick fluid.

- Turning the jar upside down is similar to turning your head upside down, which causes the otoliths to be pulled down by gravity through the jellylike material in the maculae.

Diagram B represents the body activity that would cause gravity to pull the otoliths in the inner ear downward.

17
In and Out
Why Breathing Is Essential to Life

What You Need to Know

Breathing is something that most of the time you pay no attention to. Yet, breathing is essential for life. If you were to stop breathing, the brain would suffer irreversible damage after about three or four minutes. If breathing continued to fail, death would follow.

Breathing is important because it brings in **oxygen** (O_2), a colorless gas in the air that is needed by every cell in the body. Oxygen is carried by the blood to the cells, where some of it combines with a "fuel" from digested **carbohydrates** (sugars and starches), called **glucose**. Glucose is a small sugar molecule that your body manufactures from the food you eat. In the cells, glucose combines with oxygen to produce carbon dioxide (CO_2), water (H_2O), and energy. This energy provides

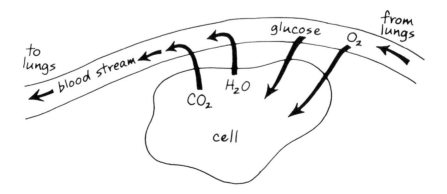

power for body activities and thus keeps you alive. The carbon dioxide and some of the water pass through the walls of the cells and enter the blood, which transports these waste gases to the lungs, where you breathe them out.

Your **breathing rate** is determined by the number of times you **inhale** (bring gases into the lungs) and exhale (expel gases from the lungs) in one minute. Normally, you inhale from one to two seconds and exhale from two to three seconds. This cycle creates a breathing rate of about 14 to 15 breaths per minute. After exercising, the breathing rate can increase to more than 100 breaths per minute.

While you can consciously increase or decrease your breathing rate, you could not do this 24 hours a day, year in and year out. Thus, an automatic controlling system is necessary. This is performed by a part of your brain called the medulla. Impulses are sent to the medulla as signals from your body that the oxygen supply in the cells is too low and the amount of carbon dioxide is too high. These messages trigger your breathing mechanism, causing your rate and depth of breathing to increase. This results in excess carbon dioxide being released and oxygen taken in by the body. This regulating mechanism keeps the carbon dioxide and oxygen levels within limits tolerable for life. For more information about the role of the medulla in controlling your breathing mechanism, see chapter 4.

Your body, like most bodies, is adapted to live at or near sea level. At high altitudes the air becomes thinner and has less pressure, making breathing more difficult. The bodies of people who live in very high altitudes have adapted to the thin air. Their lung capacity is larger, and they have an increased number of red blood cells to carry more oxygen.

If you dive under water to depths greater than approximately 130 feet (40 m), the pressure on your body increases, resulting in nitrogen (N_2) from air inside the lungs being taken into your blood. If you rise to the surface very slowly, there is sufficient time for the nitrogen to be removed from your blood and be exhaled. But if you quickly rise to the surface, these bubbles do not have time to leave the blood. As you near the water's surface, the pressure decreases and the nitrogen in your blood expands, causing pain, especially in your joints. This condition is called "the bends" because the natural reaction to relieve the pain is to bend the joints.

Exercises

Study the charts and answer these questions:

1. Which has more carbon dioxide, inhaled or exhaled air?

2. Does the amount of nitrogen in inhaled and exhaled air differ?

3. How much of the oxygen inhaled remains in the body?

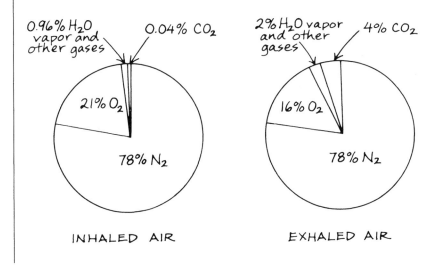

Activity: FOGGER

Purpose To collect one of the gases in your breath.

Materials paper towel
hand mirror

Procedure

1. Use the paper towel to clean and dry the mirror.

2. Hold the mirror near, but not touching, your mouth.

3. Exhale onto the mirror two or three times.

4. Examine the surface of the mirror.

Results The mirror becomes fogged.

Why?   **Respiration** is the process by which oxygen combines with glucose to produce energy and two waste byproducts, carbon dioxide and **water vapor** (water in the form of a gas). The word and picture equations for this biochemical reaction are shown below.

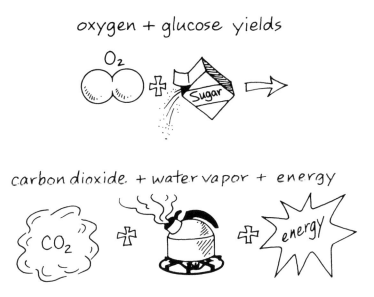

Respiration is constantly occurring in each of your cells. The water you see on the mirror is the water vapor produced by the respiration reaction inside your cells. When the warm water vapor comes in contact with the cool mirror, **condensation** (a process by which a gas loses heat energy and turns to a liquid) occurs because the mirror is colder than the inside of your lungs.

Solutions to Exercises

1. *Think!*

   • The percentage of carbon dioxide inhaled is 0.04 percent.

- The percentage of carbon dioxide exhaled is 4 percent.

Exhaled air has a higher percentage of carbon dioxide.

2. *Think!*

- The amount of nitrogen in inhaled and exhaled air is 78 percent.

No, the percentage of nitrogen in inhaled and exhaled air does not differ.

3. *Think!*

- Inhaled air contains 21 percent oxygen.
- Exhaled air contains 16 percent oxygen.
- The difference between the percentage of oxygen in inhaled air and that in exhaled air is: $21\% - 16\% = 5\%$.

Five percent of the oxygen inhaled remains in the body.

18
Travelers

The Journey of Gases In and Out of Your Lungs

What You Need to Know

Normally, you breathe through your nose. The air you breathe may be dirty, dry, too cold, or too hot. Inside the nose are hairs and mucus, which trap unwanted particles such as dust and pollen that are sometimes mixed with the air that enters your nose. Another way your body removes any irritating particles from the nose is to **sneeze**. This action forces a burst of air out of the lungs through the nose at a speed of up to about 100 miles (161 km) per hour.

Dry air is moistened by the mucus, and the temperature of the air entering the nose is warmed or cooled by the blood vessels lining the nasal cavity. Breathing through your mouth can bring air to your lungs, that is neither cleaned, moistened, nor warmed.

Air leaves the nose and moves down the back of the pharynx, where it enters the trachea. **Cilia** (microscopic hairlike structures) and mucus line the trachea and lower breathing passages. With a sweeping motion, the cilia move unwanted particles stuck in the sticky mucus back upward toward the nose or mouth, where they are sneezed or coughed out or swallowed. Coughing, like sneezing, is a gust of strong air currents coming up from the lungs to transport irritating particles out of the body. The air sneezed or coughed out can spread millions of germs to other people who inhale them. Colds are spread this way.

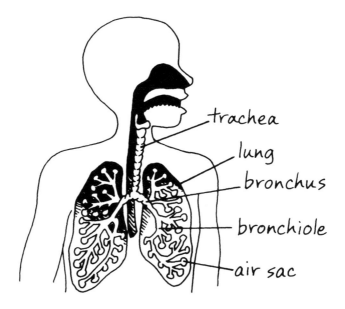

trachea
lung
bronchus
bronchiole
air sac

After passing through the trachea on the way into your body, the air goes in two directions when the trachea splits to form two tubes, called **bronchi**, leading to the lungs. Each bronchus divides many times, forming small tubes called **bronchioles**. At the end of each bronchiole is a balloon-shaped structure called an **air sac**. The lungs contain millions of these tiny air sacs, and around each air sac are many capillaries.

The membranes of the air sacs and capillaries are thin enough to allow an exchange of gases through them. Oxygen in the air inside the air sacs moves into the capillaries, and carbon dioxide moves from the capillaries into the air sacs. Oxygen travels through the blood vessels to every cell in the body, where it is used to produce energy. Waste from the cells, such as carbon dioxide and water, is carried by the blood vessels back to the air sacs. When you exhale, these waste materials are pushed up through the air passages and out your nose or mouth.

Exercises

Study the two diagrams to answer the following questions:

1. Which of the two diagrams represents an action that removes from air passages irritating particles that could damage the lungs?

2. Which diagram represents an action that brings in irritating particles that can damage the lungs?

3. Which of the diagrams represent an action that could cause harm to other people?

Activity: LUNG MODEL

Purpose To construct a model of a lung.

Materials scissors
2-liter soda bottle
9-inch (22.5-cm) round balloon
plastic trash bag
masking tape
rubber band
adult helper

Procedure

1. Ask an adult helper to cut off and discard the bottom of the soda bottle.

2. Put the balloon inside the bottle, stretching the mouth of the balloon over the mouth of the bottle.

3. Cut a 12-by-12 inch (30-by-30 cm) square sheet of plastic from the trash bag.

4. Fold the plastic sheet in half twice.

5. Beginning at the folded corner, twist a 1-inch (2.5-cm) section of the plastic sheet, and secure it with tape. This section will be called the handle.

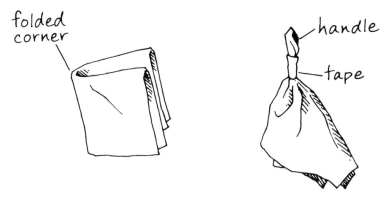

6. Lay the plastic sheet on a table and unfold it with the handle underneath.

7. Set the open end of the bottle on the plastic sheet.

8. Draw the edges of the plastic sheet up around the bottle, and secure them with the rubber band.

9. Hold the bottle with one hand and, with your other hand, move the surface of the plastic sheet out and in by pulling and pushing on the handle. Watch what happens to the balloon.

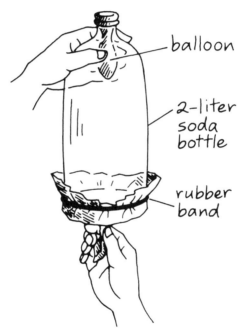

Results   The balloon inflates and deflates as the handle is pulled out and pushed in.

Why?   You have two lungs located in your chest. The diaphragm is a sheetlike muscle separating your chest from your abdomen. When the diaphragm moves down, your chest cavity enlarges and the air pressure inside decreases. When the air pressure inside your chest is less than that outside your body, air rushes into your lungs. This movement of air into the lungs is called **inspiration**. The model of the lung behaves in a similar way. When the plastic sheet over the bottom is pulled down, air rushes in and fills the balloon.

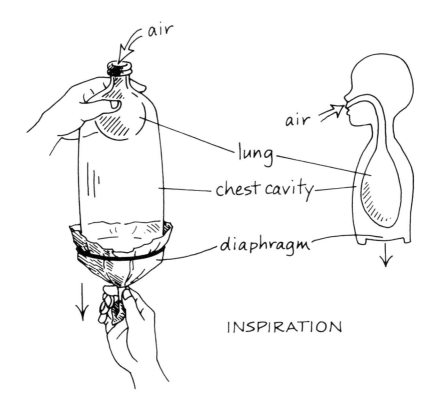

INSPIRATION

When the diaphragm moves up, your chest cavity decreases in size and the air pressure inside increases. Now the pressure inside your chest is greater than outside your body, so air is forced out of your lungs. This movement of air out of the lungs is called **expiration**.

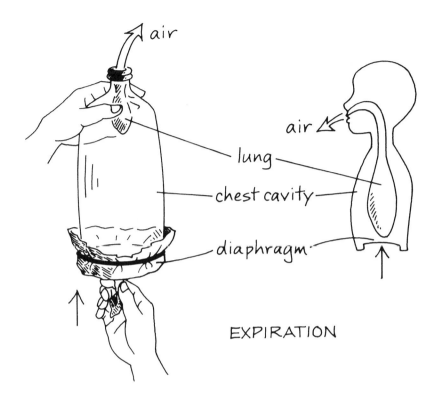

EXPIRATION

Solutions to Exercises

1. *Think!*

- A sneeze is a rapid burst of air from the lungs and out the nose.

- Sneezing is an automatic reaction that blows irritating particles out of the nose.

Diagram B represents an action that removes irritating particles that could damage the lungs.

2. *Think!*

   • Burning tobacco produces chemicals that irritate the breathing passages.

   • These chemicals make the cilia less efficient so that damaging particles in the smoke are able to get into the lungs.

   Diagram A represents an action that brings in irritating particles that can damage the lungs.

3. *Think!*

   • The smoke from the burning tobacco and the smoke exhaled by the smoker contain chemicals that are damaging not only to the smoker but to other people who might inhale them.

   • If a person has a cold, the air sneezed out can carry millions of germs. If someone breathes in this air, they could catch a cold.

   Both of the diagrams represent an action that could cause harm to other people.

19

Around and Around

How Blood Moves through Your Body

What You Need to Know

The **circulatory system** includes the heart, blood, and blood vessels. The main function of this group of body parts is to carry oxygen and nutrients to, and pick up waste from, the cells. The diagram shows blood leaving the heart and traveling through the body and back to the heart. The circulatory system gets its name from the fact that its path is like a circle that goes around and around with no beginning or end. It takes about one minute for your blood to make a complete circle when you are sitting still.

About 55 percent of your blood is made up of a clear yellow liquid, called **plasma**. Plasma is a combination of water, proteins, and salts. Digested food substances and waste materials are transported in the plasma. The remaining 45 percent of your blood is made of blood cells and **platelets**, which are not really blood cells but tiny fragments of cells. Chemicals from the platelets cause threadlike fibers, called **fibrin**, to form at the site of a wound and stop blood from escaping through the cut. This process of sealing wounds to prevent blood loss is called **blood clotting**.

Each drop of blood contains about 6 ½ million blood cells. There are two different kinds of blood cells, red and white. The

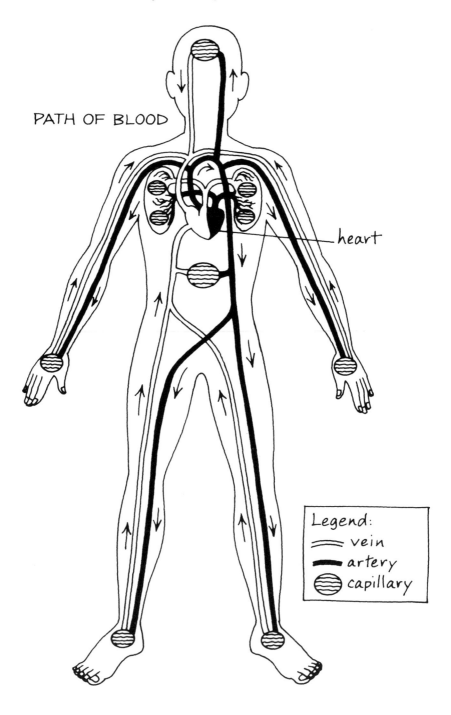

PATH OF BLOOD

heart

Legend:
≡ vein
━ artery
◍ capillary

red cells give blood its color. They are disc shaped and carry oxygen to, and remove carbon dioxide from, cells. Their color is reddest when carrying oxygen. They are the most numerous of the two blood cells. There are about 1,000 red blood cells to every white blood cell. They work for about 120 days and then wear out and are destroyed. The body makes more red blood cells to replace the old ones.

White blood cells are actually colorless and usually larger than red cells. These are the body's defenders. They squeeze out of the blood vessels to fight against intruders, such as germs or any unwanted organism that enters the body. There are different kinds of white blood cells. Some release chemicals that can kill intruders, while others absorb an intruder. White cells that die in the fight appear as pus in a wound.

There are about 100,000 miles (160,000 km) of blood vessels that transport blood around your body. There are three kinds of blood vessels. The first kind of vessel, called an artery, carries oxygen-rich blood away from the heart. The walls of arteries are thick with muscle tissue that pushes the blood along. The walls of arteries are able to stretch as the blood is pumped through them. The arteries connected to the heart are very large. Farther away from the heart, they branch out like a tree, becoming smaller and smaller at each branch.

Blood in the smallest arteries flows into the second kind of vessel, called capillaries, the smallest blood vessels. Capillaries are so tiny that red blood cells must line up single file to pass through them. In capillaries, oxygen is transferred to the body tissues and carbon dioxide is picked up by the blood.

Blood moves out of capillaries and into the third kind of vessel, called veins, which carry blood lacking oxygen back to the heart. Tiny veins join together along the way to form larger and larger veins, the largest of which is connected to the heart. Veins are different from arteries in that they do not have thick muscular walls.

It is much harder for blood to flow back to the heart, because gravity is pulling it downward. Veins have **valves,** which act like doors that let blood pass through in one direction only. Around veins are muscles that contract when you move, squeezing the veins and pushing the blood upward.

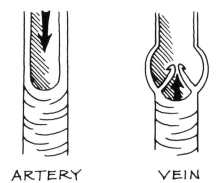

ARTERY   VEIN

Exercises

1. Study the diagram that shows the flow of blood to and from the heart, then name each blood vessel.

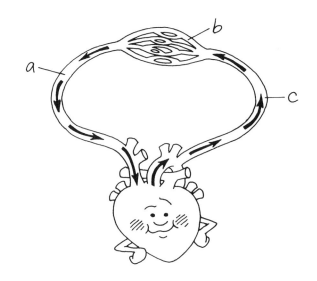

2. The blood vessel in the diagram has red blood cells moving through it. Name the vessel.

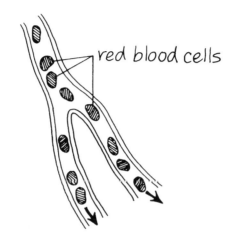

Activity: STOPPERS

Purpose To simulate the formation of blood clots.

Materials scissors
  stiff paper (a file folder will work well)
  clear drinking glass
  paper hole-punch
  1 sheet each of red, white, and yellow construction
    paper
  cotton ball

Procedure

1. Cut a square piece of stiff paper large enough to rest on top of the glass.

2. Fold the piece of stiff paper in half, and cut a notch from the center of the folded edge. The notch should be about 1 inch (2.5 cm) wide and ½ inch (1.25 cm) long.

3. Unfold the paper and place it across the top of the glass.

4. Use the hole-punch to cut 10 full circles each from the red and white paper and 10 semicircles from the edge of the yellow paper.

5. Hold half of the paper pieces of each color about 2 inches (5 cm) above the hole in the paper, then drop them.

6. Pull a small piece from the cotton ball and stretch it across the hole in the paper so that a thin layer of cotton fibers covers the hole.

7. Hold the remaining paper pieces about 2 inches (5 cm) above the covered hole in the paper, then release them.

Results   Without the cotton fibers covering the hole, the paper pieces fall through the hole. With the fibers, the paper pieces stack together on the fibers and do not fall through.

Why?   The hole in the paper represents a cut in your skin. A break in the skin usually breaks the wall of one or more blood vessels. The blood flows out the opening, and the body begins an emergency procedure of plugging this hole. Strands of fibrin are formed. Like the fibers of the cotton ball, these strands weave a web across the opening that traps the red and white blood cells and platelets, represented by the colored pieces of construction paper. A blood clot is formed. The hardened clot on the surface of the skin is called a **scab**.

Solutions to Exercises

1a. *Think!*

* Vessel A is carrying blood toward the heart.

Vessel A is a vein.

b. *Think!*

- Vessel B is very small and connects two other vessels.

Vessel B is a capillary.

c. *Think!*

- Vessel C carries blood away from the heart.

Vessel C is an artery.

2. *Think!*

- Which vessel is so small that red blood cells have to move single file through it?

The vessel is a capillary.

20
The Pump

How Your Heart Works

What You Need to Know

Your heart is a hollow, muscular organ that pumps blood through blood vessels throughout your body. Hearts vary in size and weight, depending on the size of the person, but on the average a person's heart is about the size of his or her two fists clenched together and, at maturity, weighs about $10^{1}/_{2}$ ounces (300 g). Your heart is located in the middle of your chest, with the bottom tip tilted a little to the left.

The heart is made up of special types of muscle found only in the heart, called **cardiac muscles**. About 70 times a minute, the cardiac muscles contract, squeezing blood out of the heart's chambers into the arteries and pushing it around your body. When the heart relaxes, blood enters the chambers through the veins. With each squeeze, or heartbeat, a little less than ⅓ cup (70 ml) of blood is pushed out of the heart. In one day, about 7,200 quarts (7,200 liters) of blood move in and out of your heart.

This magnificent pump works 24 hours a day without stopping through your whole lifetime. The cardiac muscles are the hardest working muscles in your body. The heart never rests, but it does beat faster or slower and can change how much blood is pumped with each beat, depending on the needs of your body. The changes in the rate of the heartbeat are controlled by your brain.

The right and left sides of your heart are actually two pumps working together. The left and right sides are separated by a type of muscular wall, called a **septum**. The right side receives blood carrying waste carbon dioxide from the body and sends it to the lungs. The left side collects oxygen-rich blood from the lungs and sends it to the body. Blood in the heart's chambers does not take away waste or bring oxygen to the heart's cells. Instead, two types of vessels, called **coronary veins** and **coronary arteries**, respectively, carry away waste and supply oxygen for the heart's cells. When coronary arteries become blocked, the muscles of the heart do not get oxygen and they die. The death of these cells is called a **heart attack**. The more cells that die, the more severe the heart attack.

Each side of the heart is divided into two chambers. The upper chamber in each side is called an **atrium**, and the lower chamber is called a **ventricle**. The diagram shows what the inside of the heart looks like. The valves allow blood to pass in one direction when it leaves any of the chambers. When the heart muscle relaxes, blood flows through the open valves from the atriums into the ventricles. When the heart contracts, the flap is closed with a thump. The valve prevents the blood from

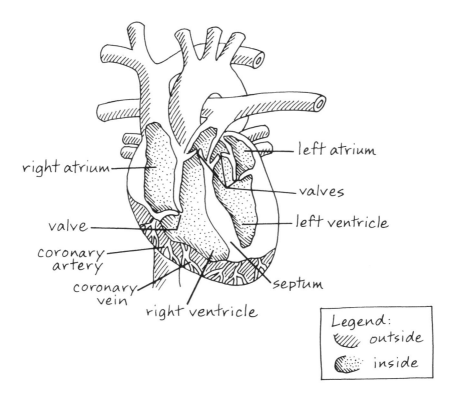

right atrium

left atrium

valves

valve

left ventricle

coronary
artery

coronary
vein

septum

right ventricle

Legend:
///// outside
inside

moving back into the atrium and directs it out of the heart through another opening. The opening and closing of the valves produces a "lub-dub" sound that can be heard through the tissues of the body.

Exercises

Study the diagram on page 154 to answer the following questions:

1. Name the chambers that contain blood with oxygen.

2. Name the chambers that are contracting and pushing blood out of the heart.

3. Name the chamber that pumps blood to the lungs.

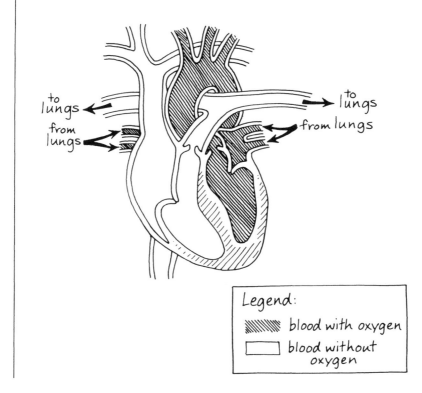

Activity: HEARTBEAT

Purpose To measure your heart rate.

Materials watch with second hand
    paper
    pencil

Procedure

1. Lay your arm on a table with the palm of your hand up.

2. Place the fingertips of your other hand below the thumb on your upturned wrist.

3. Gently press until you can feel your heartbeat.

   NOTE: You may have to move your fingertips around the area until you feel your heartbeat.

4. Count the number of heartbeats that you feel in 1 minute.

5. Repeat the procedure and record the results after different activities, such as watching television, walking, and eating.

6. Compare the results.

Results   A steady beating is felt by the fingertips. There are fewer beats per minute with more restful activities, such as watching television or eating. Doing more energetic activities, such as walking, increases the number of beats per minute.

Why?   The number of times your heart beats in one minute is called your heart rate. Adults have an average heart rate of about 70 beats per minute when sitting quietly. Children usually have a faster rate. The rate for both children and adults increases with activity because your cells need more oxygen and food when you are more active. The heart beats faster to bring more blood with these needed supplies to the cells. Strenuous activities, such as running, could cause the rate to be 150 times a minute.

Each time the heart contracts, blood is forced through the arteries. The blood moves at a rhythmic rate, causing the arteries to pulsate, or throb. The beat you feel with your finger-tips is called your **pulse**. All blood vessels have this throbbing motion, but the vessels in the wrist are close to the surface of the skin. Thus, the pulse can be felt more easily in the wrist.

Solutions to Exercises

1. *Think!*

   • The legend shows blood with oxygen as shaded.

   • Which chambers are shaded?

   The left atrium and left ventricle contain blood with oxygen.

2. *Think!*

   • When a heart chamber contracts, the valve leading out of the chamber opens.

   • Find the open valves. What are the names of the chambers below the valves?

   The left and right ventricles are contracting and pushing blood out of the heart.

3. *Think!*

- Follow back into the heart the blood vessels leading to the lungs.
- Into which chamber do these vessels lead?

The right ventricle pumps blood to the lungs.

21
Food Processor

How Your Digestive System Works

What You Need to Know

The foods you eat, which include solids and liquids, go through a giant food processor called your **digestive system**. This system contains a group of body parts that break down your food both mechanically and chemically. This breaking down of food, called **digestion**, changes food into **nutrients**, or microscopic building blocks that can be used by the cells for growth, repair, and energy. One important nutrient is glucose, which the body manufactures from the digestion of carbohydrates. The energy in glucose is changed to a form that can be used by the body. For more information about how your body makes and uses glucose, see chapter 17.

Your digestive system is constantly making new nutrients and breaking down old nutrients, which are removed as waste. Worn-out or damaged body cells are constantly being removed and replaced by new ones. For this cycle to occur day after day, you must constantly provide the starting materials—food—by eating proper amounts and kinds of foods every day.

As food travels through your digestive system, it must be broken into nutrient particles small enough to be absorbed into your bloodstream for delivery to every cell in your body. In an adult, food travels through about 30 feet (9 m) of tubing, a distance about as long as two cars. The starting point of the journey is your mouth. When food is eaten, knifelike teeth in the front of your mouth, called **incisors**, cut and slice the food. Then, grinding teeth on each side of your mouth, called **molars**, mash the food and blend it with saliva.

when you swallow this food-saliva mixture, your tongue helps to shape it into a ball known as a **bolus.** The tongue then pushes the bolus into your pharynx. To prevent food from "going down the wrong way" when you swallow, you must stop breathing and talking. A flap of cartilage called the **epiglottis** automatically closes the opening to your trachea, and the soft palate moves up and closes off the nasal passage.

All openings are closed during swallowing, except the one leading to the **esophagus.** The esophagus is a strong muscular tube, about 10 inches (25 cm) long in an adult, leading from the pharynx to the stomach. The bollus does not fall down the esophagus but is pushed down the tube by **peristalsis** (waves of muscle contractions inside the body to move substances along). This involuntary movement takes about five to ten seconds. Gravity pulls the bolus down, but even in space, where there is no gravity, astronauts are able to swallow their food due to the peristaltic action in their esophagus.

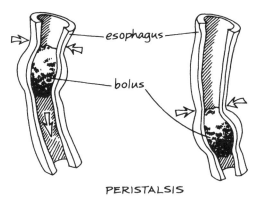

PERISTALSIS

The bolus enters the **stomach,** where it stays for two to six hours. During this time the bolus is churned into small pieces and mixed with **gastric juices,** which change the solid food to liquid. This liquid mixture, called **chyme** (pronounced "kime"), leaves the stomach and enters the **small intestine,** where more juices are added. Nutrients from the liquified food pass through the wall of the small intestine and into the bloodstream. Your small intestine is about 13 feet to 17 feet (4 m to 6 m) long and 1 inch to 1.6 inches (2.5 cm to 4 cm) wide. This long tube coils around and fits inside your abdomen.

The digested food that does not pass through the wall of the small intestine enters a larger, wider tube, called the **large intestine**. Water is taken out of the food, and the remains are temporarily stored in the **colon** (lower part of the large intestine) until they are passed from the body as waste. Your large intestine is about 5 feet to 6 feet (1.5 m to 2 m) long and varies in width, but is about twice as wide as the small intestine. The basic parts of the food canal—the mouth, esophagus, stomach, small intestine, large intestine, and colon—are shown in the diagram.

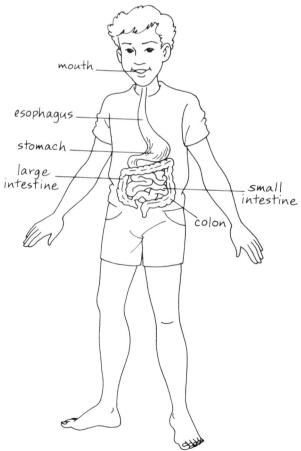

mouth

esophagus

stomach

large intestine

small intestine

colon

Exercises

Compare each action with the diagram that best symbolizes it:

1. Peristalsis

2. Mixing of ground food with saliva

3. Biting into a slice of cheese

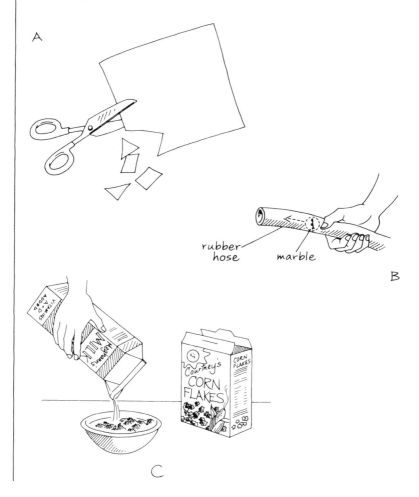

Activity: OVERFLOW

Purpose   To demonstrate the squeezing of food from the stomach into the small intestine.

Materials   tube of toothpaste
3-ounce (90-ml) paper cup

Procedure

1. Hold the tube of toothpaste in your hands.

2. With the cap screwed on tight, position the tube above the paper cup as in the diagram.

3. Moving your fingers, squeeze the tube in different places.

4. Remove the cap from the tube and squeeze the tube with your fingers.

Results   With the cap secured, the toothpaste inside the tube moves around in, but remains inside, the tube. Without the cap, the toothpaste moves out the opening in the tube.

Why?   Your stomach has three layers of muscles contracting in different directions. These squeezing actions, like those of your hands, thoroughly mash the food in your stomach and mix it with digestive juices, forming a soupy paste. Between your stomach and the **duodenum** (upper part of your small intestine closest to the stomach), there is a muscle called the **sphincter**. When the sphincter relaxes, it opens and a small

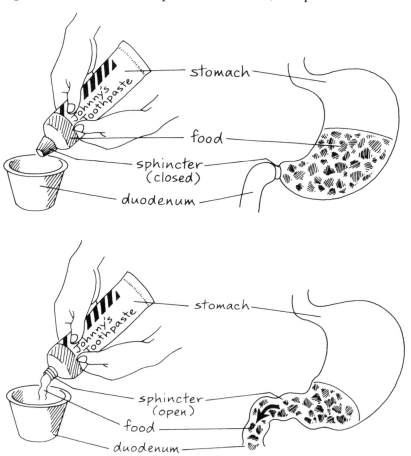

amount of food is squeezed into the duodenum, just as tooth-paste moves out of the tube when the cap is off.

After a small amount of food leaves the stomach, the sphincter quickly closes, sealing off the passageway. The rest of the food remains in the stomach until the duodenum is ready to receive it. This removal of food from the stomach prevents food from filling the stomach and pushing up into the lower part of the esophagus. Because the gastric juices in the stomach are acidic, an overflow could damage the tissue of the esophagus and cause a burning pain called "heartburn."

Solutions to Exercises

1. *Think!*

   - Peristalsis is the movement of the bolus through the esophagus.

   - The esophagus is squeezed by contracting muscles behind the bolus to move the food forward.

   Diagram B best symbolizes peristalsis.

2. *Think!*

   - Saliva is a liquid inside the mouth.

   - Food ground by the teeth is made soft by mixing it with saliva.

   Diagram C best symbolizes the mixing of ground food with saliva.

3. *Think!*

   - Food is cut or sliced by the knife-shaped teeth in the front of the mouth called incisors.

   Diagram A best symbolizes biting into a slice of cheese.

22
Support System

How Your Bones Keep You Together

What You Need to Know

All the bones of your body make up the **skeletal system**. This system provides the framework that allows you to stand upright and also protects delicate internal body parts. An adult has about 206 bones. The number of bones varies from person to person because of the differences in the number of small bones in the hands and feet. The bones are distributed in this way: skull, 29; spine, 26; ribs and breastbone, 25; shoulders, arms, and hands, 64; pelvis, legs, and feet, 62. The central support for your entire body is your spine. It is made up of 26 linked bones, called **vertebrae**, which become progressively larger down your back.

Bones are constructed to be strong yet light. They have a stretching strength almost as strong as that of cast iron, and weight for weight are stronger than steel or reinforced concrete. Bones have different shapes depending on the work they do, but all are made of the same material. The thin, tough outer layer of bones is called the **periosteum**. If a bone breaks, it is this layer that multiplies and grows over the break, joining the two parts together again.

Under the periosteum is hard, compact bone composed of living bone cells that encircle tiny canals called **haversian canals**. Blood vessels carry food and oxygen through the haversian canals to the bone cells. The inner part of the bone looks like a honeycomb and is often called "spongy bone." Some

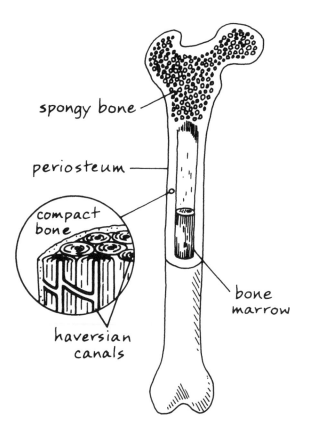

spongy bone

periosteum

compact bone

haversian canals

bone marrow

bones contain soft tissue, called **bone marrow**, which makes red blood cells.

The place where bones meet is called a **joint**. The bones are held together by tough, straplike strands of connective tissue called **ligaments** and muscles. The ends of the bones are covered with cartilage. The joints are surrounded by a capsule of thin, slippery material that produces a lubricating liquid. The cartilage and lubricant prevent the bones from grinding together. Some people are said to be "double-jointed." No one has multiple joints, but they can have extra long ligaments in their joints, which allow them to bend farther than usual.

Exercises

Study the description and diagram of each type of joint, then select the example, shown on page 171, that best represents the movement of each joint.

1. Ball-and-socket joint: The ball-shaped end of the thigh bone rests in a cup-shaped socket on the hip bone. The thigh can move a limited amount in all directions.

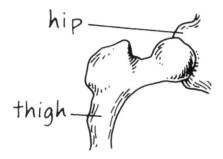

2. Hinge joint: In the elbow, the rounded end of the bone of the upper arm fits into a cradle formed by the bones of the forearm. The bones of the elbow can move back and forth in one direction.

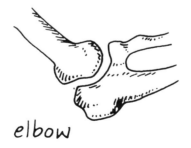

3. Pivot joint: In the neck, a ring on the underside of the vertebra at the top of the spine fits over a peg on the vertebra below it, allowing the head to pivot from side to side.

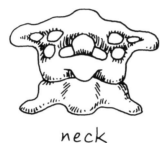

neck

4. Gliding joint: Bones in your wrist fit together like smooth puzzle pieces. Movement is accomplished as these bones glide next to one another.

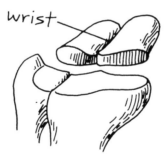

wrist

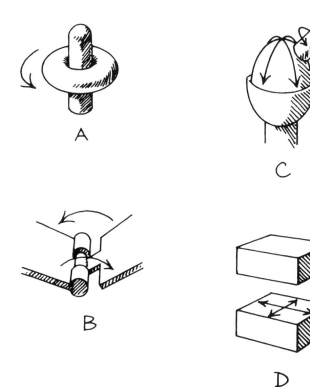

Activity: BACKBONE

Purpose To construct a model of the spine.

Materials 2 large, 2 medium, and 2 small empty thread spools
cardboard
pencil
scissors
paper hole-punch
ruler
string
tape

Procedure

1. Place the flat ends of all of the thread spools (except one of the small spools) on the cardboard.

2. Draw circles on the cardboard by tracing around the base of each spool.

3. Cut out the five paper circles from the cardboard, and use the hole-punch to make a hole in the center of each.

4. Cut an 18-inch (45-cm) length of string.

5. Thread one end of the string through the hole in one of the large spools, then tape the end of the string to the bottom of the spool.

6. Thread the free end of the string through the hole in one of the large cardboard circles.

7. Add the second large spool to the string, followed by the second large cardboard circle.

8. Add the medium-sized spools and the medium cardboard circles alternately to the string.

9. Add the small spools to the string, with the small cardboard circle between them.

10. Tape the free end of the string to the end of the small spool.

11. Stand the column of spools on a table, with the large spool on the bottom.

12. Holding the bottom spool on a table, push the top spool about 2 inches (5 cm) to one side.

13. Repeat the previous step several times, pushing the top spool in different directions.

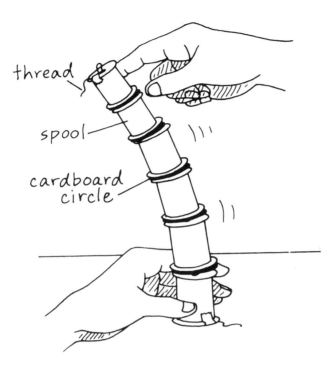

thread

spool

cardboard
circle

Results A model of the spine is made. The string of spools is able to lean in any direction.

Why? Because the vertebrae, like the thread spools, are not permanently attached together, you can lean and bend in different directions. Between each pair of vertebrae is a disk of cartilage that acts as a shock absorber, just as the cardboard circle between spools keeps them from knocking together. Without this flexible disk, the vertebrae would grind together and you would not be able to turn, twist, or bend your torso without pain and damage to vertebrae.

Like the hole in the thread spool, there is a hole in the back part of each vertebra. These holes create a passageway called the **spinal canal**, through which the nerves of the spinal cord are threaded. The diagram on page 174 compares the model with the parts of the spine.

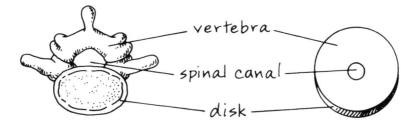

TOP VIEW

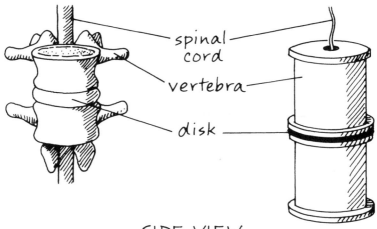

SIDE VIEW

Solutions to Exercises

1. *Think!*

- Which example most looks like a cup holding a ball with a handle?

Example C best represents the movement of a ball-and-socket joint.

2. *Think!*

   • Which example looks like a hinge?

   Example B best represents the movement of a hinge joint.

3. *Think!*

   • Which example shows a ring pivoting around a peg?

   Example A best represents the movement of a pivot joint.

4. *Think!*

   • Which example shows a smooth gliding motion be-tween two surfaces?

   Example D best represents the movement of a gliding joint.

23
Pullers

How Your Muscles Move Your Body

What You Need to Know

Your body is an amazing machine, certainly more remarkable than any devised by humans. It can run, jump, throw a baseball, or perform delicate movements, such as threading a needle or turning a page in this book. All body movements are possible because of the many different muscles in your body.

Muscles come in all shapes and sizes, depending on their location and function. You have more than 600 muscles, making up about 40 percent of your body weight. Your bones make up about 18 percent of your body weight. Bones provide the skeletal framework to which muscles are attached, but it is the muscles that move the bones and create movement.

See if you can do this: For one minute, sit so perfectly still that not a muscle in your body is moving. Could you do it? No way! That big muscle that is your heart is pumping blood, your chest is moving in and out as you breathe, your eyes have blinked about 15 times in the past minute, and many other muscles continue to move. The fact is, your body never quits moving, even when you try to stop it.

Some muscles, such as those that support your body, never completely relax. If they did, you would collapse. Do all these supportive muscles work every second of the day? No, some muscles in the group work while others rest. This keeps the entire group from being overworked.

Muscles are classified as voluntary or involuntary. Voluntary muscles are muscles that you can consciously control, such as those in your arms and legs. Involuntary muscles, such as those in your digestive tract, are not consciously controlled by you. Some muscles are both voluntary and involuntary; for example, your eyes blink automatically, but you can also make them blink.

Your muscles are made of tissue of which there are three different types: smooth, skeletal, and cardiac. Smooth muscle tissue is groups of long, unstriped cells with one nucleus; the cells are pointed at each end and are usually grouped together in flattened sheets. Smooth muscles are involuntary. They are common throughout the body, occurring in the walls of many internal body organs, such as blood vessels.

Skeletal muscle tissue is made of long, striped cells with several nuclei in each. Each cell looks like a long cylinder with dark and light bands running across it. These cells join together in bundles that are grouped together to form muscles that you feel in your arms and legs. Skeletal muscle tissue is one of the most abundant tissues in your body. Some skeletal muscles, such as those in the upper arm, are attached to bones by

MUSCLE TISSUE

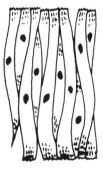 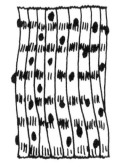 

smooth   skeletal   cardiac

tendons (tough, ropy tissue connecting muscle to bone.) Others are attached directly to bones, while some, such as the tongue, are attached to other muscles.

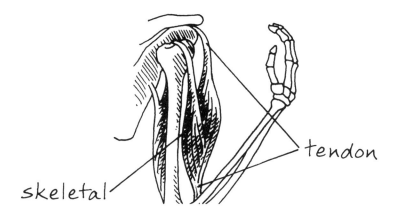

skeletal

tendon

Cardiac muscle tissue is made of cells that are striped like those of skeletal muscle tissue. However, unlike skeletal muscle tissue, it has branching fibers and experiences rhythmic involuntary contractions. Cardiac tissue cells are so tightly packed together that it is hard to tell one cell from the other. This special tissue is found only in the muscles of the heart. Like smooth muscles, cardiac muscles are involuntary. Your heart works hard to pump blood continuously during your whole life. Cardiac tissue has the strength and endurance the heart needs.

When muscles work, they contract; that is, they get shorter and thicker. Muscles can only pull, they cannot push. This is why many skeletal muscles, like those in the upper arm, work in pairs. One muscle, called a **flexor**, works by pulling on a tendon to bend a joint while the other muscle relaxes. When the flexor muscle relaxes, the other muscle, called an **extensor**, pulls on a different tendon to straighten the same joint. Almost

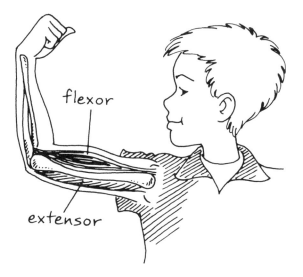

every body movement requires the use of both flexor and extensor muscles.

Exercise does not increase the number of muscles in your body, but it does make the muscles you have stronger, firmer, and larger. Not using muscles can make them weaker, flabby, and smaller. However, the size of muscles does not always indicate their strength.

Excessive exercise can cause muscles to feel sore because of the buildup of waste chemicals in the muscle tissue. Rest and warm water applied to the area will often bring relief. Muscle cramps, caused by a temporary lack of food or oxygen to muscle cells, also cause pain. Relaxing and rubbing the muscle usually helps.

Exercises

1. Study the two diagrams of cells, then identify the muscle cells that would be found in the walls of arteries.

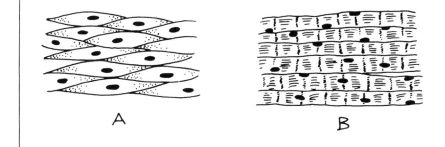

A   B

2. Select the position of the foot that would give relief from
a cramp in the calf muscle (muscle on the back of the
lower part of the leg.)

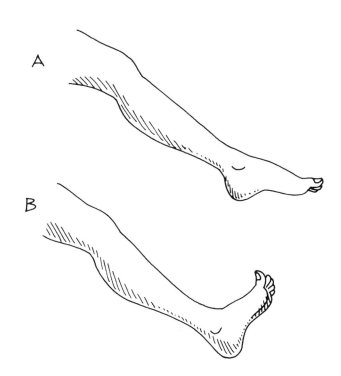

Activity: MUSCLE POWER

Purpose To locate the muscle pair in the upper arm.

Materials chair
heavy table
helper

Procedure

1. Ask your helper to sit in the chair next to the table.

2. Instruct your helper to place one of his or her hands, palm up, under the edge of the table and to try to lift the table with a medium pressure.

CAUTION: Warn your helper not to strain.

3. While pressure is being applied to the table, feel the front and back of your helper's upper arm.

4. Next, ask your helper to place his or her hand, palm down, on top of the table and to press down.

5. Again, feel the same parts of your helper's upper arm.

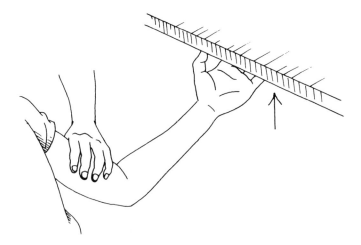

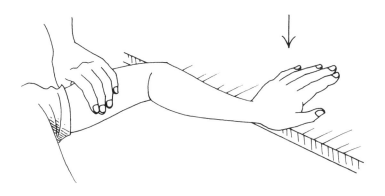

Results The muscle in front of the arm feels harder than the muscle in the back of the arm when the hand is pushing up on the table. The back muscle in the arm feels harder when the hand is pressing down on the table.

Why? Pushing up on the table causes the flexor muscle in the front of the arm to contract and harden. Pushing down on the table causes the extensor muscle in the back of the arm to contract and harden. Even though the joint in the arm (the elbow) is not being bent and straightened, the muscle pair in the upper arm causing these movements is identified in this activity.

Solutions to Exercises

1. *Think!*

- The walls of arteries contain smooth muscle cells.
- Smooth muscle cells are long, unstriped, and pointed at each end, and they have only one nucleus.

Diagram A represents muscle cells in artery walls.

2.   *Think!*

- The muscle on top of the leg must relax and the calf muscle contract to bend the ankle joint and extend the toes.

- The muscle on top of the leg must contract and the calf muscle relax to straighten the ankle joint and raise the toes.

- A cramped muscle must relax to relieve a cramp.

Diagram B shows the position of the foot that would give relief to a cramp in the calf muscle.

24
And Then There Were Three

How You Were Born

What You Need to Know

Humans are born as a result of **sexual reproduction** (the process of producing a new organism from two parents). In order for a new baby to form, a **sperm** (male sex cell) must join with an ovum (female sex cell, or egg). The joining of the ovum and sperm, called **fertilization**, takes place inside the body of the female, or mother.

Eggs from chickens and other birds are very large because they contain stored food. Human ova do not contain stored food and are very small. A human ovum is about 0.005 inch (0.013 cm) in diameter. Usually, only one ovum is released from one of the female's two **ovaries** (female organs that produce ova) each month. It then travels down the **fallopian tube** that connects the ovary to the **uterus** (organ where the baby grows and develops).

A male can produce millions of sperm each day. Sperm are even more microscopic in size than ova. A sperm is about 0.002 inch (0.005 cm) long. The head of the sperm, the largest part, contains the cell's nucleus. The sperm also has a tail that whips from side to side, helping the sperm to move and reach the ovum.

A baby starts to develop as soon as the ovum and one sperm join together to form one new cell, called a fertilized egg or

HUMAN OVUM

HUMAN SPERM

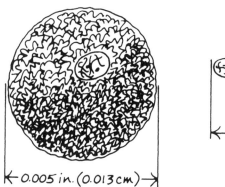

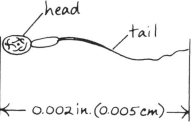

zygote. This union usually takes place in the upper part of a fallopian tube. The newly formed zygote is swept through the fallopian tube by tiny hairs that line the tubes. During the journey through the fallopian tube to the uterus, the zygote starts dividing. First, it forms two identical attached cells. Both of these cells then divide, forming four attached cells; the four divide to make eight; and so on. This rapid cell division that converts a zygote into a ball of cells is called **cleavage**. By the time the zygote reaches the uterus, it has divided five or six times, forming a hollow ball of cells filled with fluid. The unborn baby is called an **embryo** during the first two months of its development, then a **fetus** until it is born.

During its prebirth development, the baby gets food and oxygen from a special organ called the **placenta**. The placenta serves as a barrier that separates the baby's blood from the mother's blood. This organ, made partly of the mother's tissue and partly of the baby's tissue, contains blood vessels from each of them. The baby is connected to the placenta by a flexible tissue called the **umbilical cord**.

Food and oxygen from the mother's blood move from the placenta through the umbilical cord to the baby. Waste from the baby's body passes through the cord and placenta into the mother's blood. These wastes are then removed from the mother's body along with her own waste products. You can look at your belly button and see where your umbilical cord was attached. During **pregnancy** (the condition of carrying an unborn baby), the amount of blood in the mother may increase from approximately seven pints to ten pints in order to provide nourishment for the baby.

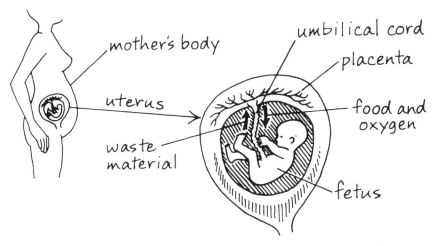

During the baby's nine-month growth period, the uterus changes from its normal pear shape and size to a size larger than a basketball. At about four weeks old, the embryo has a pumping heart, and the beginning development of eyes, arms, and legs is evident. At five weeks, fingers are faintly suggested. At three months, the fetus lives in a fluid-filled sac and has all major organ systems. At five months, the fetus looks much like it will at birth. It kicks its legs and swims around inside its watery environment and even hiccups. It sleeps, hears noises, explores its environment with its hands, and even sucks its thumb. Approximately six weeks after birth, the uterus finally returns to its normal size.

At the end of the nine months of development, the baby is born. During the birthing process, the muscles in the uterus contract to push the baby out through the opening in the uterus. The fluid-filled sac surrounding the baby breaks, and the baby moves from the uterus through the passageway called the

vagina and out the mother's body. Babies are usually born head first. With a cry, the baby takes its first breath of air. The doctor ties and cuts the umbilical cord, and the newborn baby is now ready to begin its life outside its mother's body.

A baby is usually about 20 inches (50.8 cm) long at birth and about 30 inches (76.2 cm) long at age 1. At birth, a baby's head makes up a quarter of its total length and looks huge in comparison to the rest of its body. This is because a baby's brain is well developed at birth; by age 2, the brain is almost adult size. By the time the person has reached adulthood, the head will only be approximately one-eighth of the total body length.

Exercises

1. If the mother produces two ova, each of which is fertilized by different sperm, and each zygote develops into a baby, the babies are called nonidentical, or **fraternal, twins**. When one ovum is fertilized and the dividing zygote splits in two, and each half develops into a baby, **identical twins** will be born. Study the diagrams and determine which shows the development of identical twins.

CLEAVAGE

A

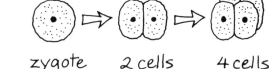

zygote   2 cells   4 cells

CLEAVAGE

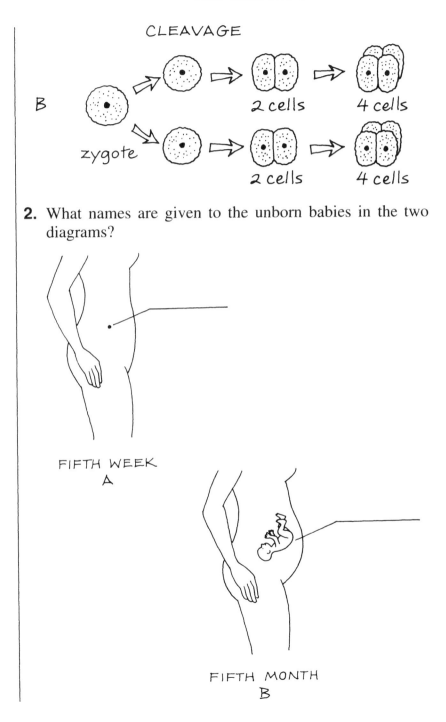

B

zygote

2 cells

4 cells

2 cells

4 cells

2. What names are given to the unborn babies in the two diagrams?

FIFTH WEEK
A

FIFTH MONTH
B

Activity: BOY OR GIRL

Purpose   To determine the odds of a baby being a boy or a girl.

Materials   masking tape
marking pen
2 coffee cups
15 red kidney beans
5 white lima beans
compass
sheet of typing paper

Procedure

1. Use the tape and marking pen to label one cup "ova" and the other cup "sperm."

2. Place 10 red kidney beans in the cup labeled "ova" and 5 red kidney beans in the cup labeled "sperm."

3. Add 5 white lima beans to the sperm cup and thoroughly mix the beans.

4. Set the cups on a table.

5. Use the compass to draw ten separate circles with a 2-inch (5-cm) diameter on the paper.

6. Place the paper on the table near the cups.

7. Without looking into the cups, take one bean out of each and place the two beans in one of the circles drawn on the paper.

8. Continue taking one bean out of each cup and placing the pairs in a circle until both cups are empty.

Results   Each circle has two beans in it. Half the circles have two red beans, and half have one red and one white bean.

Why?   The sex of a baby is due to two sets of instructions. These instructions are in the sex chromosomes, known as X and Y. Females have two X chromosomes, and males have an X and a Y. Ova and sperm have one sex chromosome each. Ova have only X chromosomes, while half of the sperm have X chromosomes and half have Y chromosomes. If an ovum is fertilized by a sperm carrying a Y chromosome, the XY combination produces a boy. If the ovum is fertilized by a sperm carrying an X chromosome, the XX combination produces a girl.

The red beans in this experiment represent X chromosomes, and the white beans Y chromosomes. The combination of two red beans indicates a girl, and a red-and-white combination a boy. The sex chromosome from the sperm determines the sex of the baby. As with the random combination of the beans, the odds of having a boy or a girl baby are 50-50.

Solutions to Exercises

1. *Think!*

- Identical twins develop when the zygote splits into two separate parts.

Diagram B shows the development of identical twins.

2a. *Think!*

- The unborn baby is five weeks old.
- What name is given to an unborn baby up to two months old?

Diagram A is of an embryo.

b. *Think!*

- The unborn baby is five months old.
- What name is given to an unborn baby from two months until birth?

Diagram B is of a fetus.

25
Pass It On

Where You Got Those Eyes

What You Need to Know

What do you look like? Are you short or tall? Is your hair dark or blond? Are your eyes brown or blue? Your height, hair and eye color, and many other things about your appearance are called **traits** (characteristics that help to identify living organisms).

Children usually look like their parents or grandparents in some ways. This is because parents pass on their traits to their offspring. The passing on of traits from parent to child is called **heredity**, and the traits being passed on are called **inherited traits**. The study of heredity is called **genetics**. The Austrian **botanist** (scientist who studies plants) Gregor Mendel (1822–1884) is called the father of genetics because he was the first scientist to study inherited traits.

Mendel studied the inherited traits of peas. The information that he learned about inherited traits in plants has been compared to inherited traits in humans. Babies, like peas, receive traits from their parents during fertilization. Human fertilization is when a sperm joins an ovum to form a zygote (see chapter 24). The zygote has chromosomes from the father and mother. Each chromosome is made up of **genes** that determine all your inherited traits. Every offspring has two genes for each trait—one from the father and one from the mother.

Mendel's studies helped scientists answer questions such as why parents with dimpled chins can have a child without a dimple. He discovered that when the two genes from parents join, one gene determines the trait in the offspring. A gene that, when present, determines the trait of an offspring is called a **dominant gene**. A gene that does not determine the trait when a dominant gene is present is called a **recessive gene**.

Study the diagram below to see how the presence or absence of a dimpled chin is inherited. Capital letters are used for a dominant gene and lowercase letters for recessive genes. The gene for a dimpled chin, identified by a D, is dominant. The gene for a chin without a dimple, identified by a d, is recessive. The three possible combinations of genes are DD, Dd, and dd. The combinations DD and dd are called **pure traits** because both genes are identical. Dd has two unlike genes and is called a **hybrid**. Both the pure chin dimple (DD) and the hybrid chin dimple (Dd) produce an offspring with a dimple. In the hybrid chin dimple (Dd), the dominant D gene cancels out the recessive d gene. When a gene for a chin without a dimple is received from both parents (dd), the offspring receives this pure trait and does not have a dimpled chin.

People are not just short or tall. Some are very tall, some very short, and some medium. This tells us that there are not just dominant and recessive genes. Some genes are neither domi-

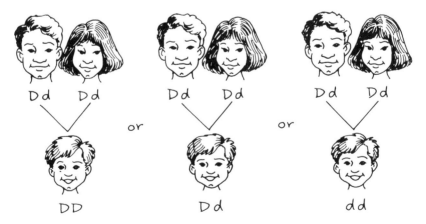

nant nor recessive. When these genes combine, their traits blend together. There are genes for skin and eye color as well as genes for many other traits that blend together. Most of your traits come not from one gene but from a special combination of many different genes. This is why even people with the same parents can be so different.

A **Punnett square** is a method of showing all the possible gene combinations that are transferred from parents to offspring. For example, consider the combination of genes from one parent with genes for pure brown eyes (BB) and the other with genes for hybrid brown eyes (Bb). B is the dominant gene for brown eyes, and b the recessive gene for blue eyes.

There are four possible combinations because each parent has two genes. Each box in the square contains a combination of letters corresponding to the letters above and to the left of the square. The number of boxes with the same gene combination tells what percentage of the offspring will most probably have that eye color. One box out of 4 is 25 percent; 2 out of 4 is 50 percent; 3 out of 4 is 75 percent; and 4 out of 4 is 100 percent.

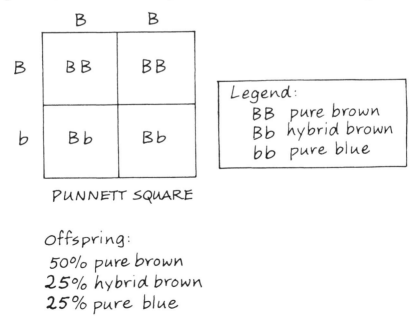

PUNNETT SQUARE

Legend:
BB pure brown
Bb hybrid brown
bb pure blue

Offspring:
50% pure brown
25% hybrid brown
25% pure blue

Exercises

1. The children in the diagram are brother and sister. Study the traits of the children and adults, then determine which pair of adults are the parents of the children.

2. From the moment of fertilization, the number of chromosomes in the cells of humans is 46. Sperm and ova are reproductive cells, and each has half as many chromosomes as body cells do. What would be the number of chromosomes of each of the cells in the diagram?

HUMAN FERTILIZATION

sperm   ovum   zygote

3. The ability to roll the edges of one's tongue into a U shape is a dominant human trait. Use a Punnett square to determine the percentage of offspring that can roll their tongues if both parents have hybrid genes for tongue rolling (Tt).

Activity: COIN TOSS

Purpose   To compare the chances of a coin toss to the combinations produced in a Punnett square.

Materials   masking tape
2 pennies
marking pen
pencil
ruler
sheet of typing paper
small hand towel

Procedure

1. Place one small piece of tape on the front and back of each penny.

2. Use the pen to write a capital E on one side of each penny and a lowercase e on the other side.

3. Use the pencil, ruler, and paper to prepare the following chart.

COIN TOSS RESULTS		
	Trial 1	Trial 2	Trial 3
EE			
Ee			
ee			

4. Stretch the towel out on a table.

   NOTE: The towel will prevent the coins from rolling off the table in the next step.

5. Hold both coins in your hands and shake them back and forth several times, then toss the coins together over the towel.

6. Put an X on your chart under "Trial 1" and next to the letter combination that corresponds to the combination showing on the coins.

7. Toss the coins three more times, recording each letter combination under Trial 1.

8. Repeat steps 5 through 6 two more times, recording the results of each trial.

Results   In each trial, the coin toss produces variable results.

Why?   E is being used to represent a dominant gene for a
free (unattached) earlobe, and e to represent a recessive gene
for an attached earlobe. If a Punnett square were used instead
of a coin toss to predict the possible gene combinations, the
results would not vary. There would be one EE, two Ee, and
one ee. Three out of 4 combinations have the dominant gene,
E; and 1 out of 4 has two recessive genes, ee. Thus, 75 percent
of the offspring would have free earlobes and 25 percent would
have attached earlobes. Although the Punnett square shows the

possible combinations, it cannot be used to predict what actually can happen if only four children are born. As the results of this experiment show, chance affects heredity.

Solutions to Exercises

1. *Think!*

   • The children both have narrow noses, thin lips, dimple in chin, and dark eyes like parents A.

   • One child has blond hair but does not have the broader nose or fuller lips of parents B.

   Parents A are the parents of the children.

2. *Think!*

   • Human body cells have 46 chromosomes.

   • Sex cells have half as many chromosomes as body cells.

   • The zygote is a combination of the chromosomes in the sperm and ovum. The zygote has the same number of chromosomes as body cells.

   The sperm and ovum have 23 chromosomes each, and the zygote has 46.

3. *Think!*

   • The four gene combinations are TT, Tt, Tt, and tt.

- Only the pure recessive gene, tt, produces an offspring that cannot roll its tongue.

Seventy-five percent of the offspring can roll their tongues.

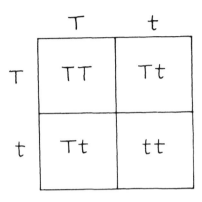

Glossary

Adam's apple: A common name for the larynx.

Air sac: A small balloon-shaped sac at the end of each bronchiole, where gases are exchanged with blood.

Anatomy: The study of the parts of the human body and their functions.

Anterior: Situated in the front.

Arteries: Blood vessels that carry oxygen-rich blood away from the heart.

Association neurons: Nerve cells in the brain and spinal cord that connect sensory neurons to motor neurons.

Atrium: One of the two upper chambers of the heart.

Auditory nerve: The main nerve connecting the ear to the brain.

Blind spot: The part of the eye where the optic nerve enters that has no rods or cones and is therefore insensitive to light.

Blood clotting: The formation of fibrin at the site of a wound to seal the wound and prevent blood loss.

Blood vessels: Pathways in the body along which blood passes when pumped by the heart. Includes arteries, veins, and capillaries.

Bolus: Food ball prepared in the mouth and swallowed.

Bone marrow: Soft tissue inside bones which makes red blood cells.

Botanist: Scientist who studies plants.

Breathing: The mechanical process of moving air into and out of the body.

Breathing rate: The number of times you inhale and exhale in one minute.

Bronchi (singular **bronchus**):   The two branches of the trachea leading to the lungs.

Bronchioles: Branches of the bronchi.

Bud pore: The opening in the top of a taste bud.

Capillaries: Tiny blood vessels that connect the small branches of arteries to the small branches of veins.

Carbohydrates: Sugars and starches that, when digested, become glucose.

Cardiac muscles: Special types of muscle found only in the heart that are the hardest working muscles in the body.

Cartilage: Firm but flexible supportive material.

Cell membrane: The thin, filmlike outer layer that holds a cell together and separates it from its environment. It allows materials to pass into and out of the cell.

Cells: The smallest units or building blocks of all living things.

Cell theory: Theory stating that all living things are made up of cells and that all cells come from previously existing cells.

Center of gravity: The point at which an object balances.

Cerebellum: Small, pear-shaped area at the base of the cerebrum that controls and coordinates voluntary movements and balance.

Cerebrum: Largest and most complex part of the brain; made of two joined hemispheres, where reasoning, memory, and senses are controlled.

Chemoreceptor: A sensory receptor that is stimulated by smell or taste.

Choroid: The second or middle layer of the eyeball, which brings food and oxygen to the eye and contains pigment that gives the eye color.

Chromosomes: Threadlike structures in the nucleus of a cell that carry instructions, much like a computer program, to make the cell work.

Chyme: Liquid food mixture that leaves the stomach and enters the small intestine.

Cilia: Microscopic hairlike structures.

Circulatory system: Group of body parts (heart, blood, and blood vessels) that carry materials to and from cells.

Cleavage: Rapid cell division that converts a zygote into a ball of cells.

Cochlea: The coiled tube in the inner ear, where mechanoreceptors for hearing are located.

Colon: The lower part of the large intestine where waste from digested food is temporarily stored until it is passed from the body.

Concentrated solution: A mixture of a small number of water molecules and a large number of dissolved particles.

Condensation: The process by which a gas loses enough heat energy to change to a liquid.

Conditioned reflex: A reflex in which a new stimulus is substituted for the original stimulus.

Cone: Light-sensitive cell in the eye that detects color images.

Conjunctiva: A thin, transparent film that covers and protects the front of the eye, and that is very sensitive to even the smallest particles of dust.

Constriction: Contraction. Blood vessels and pupils get smaller when they constrict.

Converging lenses: Lenses that bend light inward so that farsighted people can see things at a shorter distance.

Cornea: The bulging, transparent area of the sclera that covers the front of the eye.

Coronary artery: A blood vessel that carries oxygen-rich blood to the cells of the heart.

Coronary vein: A blood vessel that carries waste away from the cells of the heart.

Cortex: The layer of nerve cells that covers the two hemispheres of the cerebrum and controls the activities of the body that are governed by the hemispheres. The right side of the cortex controls activities in the left side of the body, and vice versa.

Cuticle: The thick skin around the edges of finger- or toenails.

Cytoplasm: A jellylike material made mostly of water. It fills the cell, and the other parts of the cell float in it.

Decibels: Units used to measure noise level.

Dermis: The inner layer of skin; thicker than the epidermis.

Desensitized: Insensitive or nonreactive.

Diaphragm: The large, sheetlike muscle between the chest and abdomen.

Digestion: The breaking down of food, both mechanically and chemically, into nutrients.

Digestive system: The group of body parts used in digestion.

Dilation: Expansion. Blood vessels and pupils get bigger when they dilate.

Dilute solution: A mixture containing a large number of water molecules and a small number of dissolved particles.

Diverging lenses: Lenses that bend light outward so that nearsighted people can focus at a greater distance.

Dominant gene: A gene that, when present, determines the trait of the offspring.

Duodenum: The upper part of the small intestine closest to the stomach.

Ear canal: The passage from the outer ear to the tympanic membrane.

Embryo: Unborn baby during the first two months of development.

Endoplasmic reticulum: The structure within the cell where protein is made. Protein is used for growth and repair.

Endotherms: Animals that are able to maintain a constant internal body temperature even when the temperature outside their bodies changes.

Epidermis: The thin, visible outer layer of skin.

Epiglottis: The flap of cartilage that closes the opening to the trachea to prevent food from "going down the wrong way" during swallowing.

Esophagus: The strong muscular tube that leads from the pharynx to the stomach.

Eustachian tube: A narrow tube connecting the middle ear to the throat.

Evaporation: The process by which a liquid absorbs enough heat energy to change to a gas.

Exhale: To breathe out, expelling gases from the lungs.

Expiration: Movement of air out of the lungs.

Extensor: A muscle that straightens a joint.

Fallopian tubes: Two tubes connecting the ovaries to the uterus.

Fertilization: The joining of an ovum and a sperm to form a zygote.

Fetus: Unborn baby from two months until birth.

Fibrin: Threadlike fibers that cause blood clotting.

Filtration: The passage of water and dissolved materials through the cell membrane.

Flexor: A muscle that bends a joint.

Follicle (hair):   Depression beneath the skin from which hair grows; touch sensors are often found next to a hair follicle.

Fovea: A postage stamp-size area on the retina where cones are abundant and where the eye's lens focuses light; point at which you see an object clearly.

Fraternal twins: Nonidentical twins resulting when the mother produces two ova, each of which is fertilized by different sperm, and each zygote develops into a baby.

Frequency: The number of sound waves that reach an ear in one second.

Gastric juices: A liquid in the stomach that turns solid foods into liquids.

Gene: The part of a chromosome that determines inherited traits.

Genetics: The study of heredity.

Glucose: A sugar formed by the digestion of carbohydrates that can be carried in the blood as fuel for the body.

Golgi bodies: The structure within the cell where proteins are stored until needed.

Goose bumps: Small bumps on the skin's surface as a result of contracted muscles that raise individual hairs.

Gravity: The force that pulls everything toward the earth's center.

Hard palate: The front part of the roof of the mouth.

Haversian canals: Tiny canals in the center of bone cells, through which blood vessels carry food and oxygen to bone cells.

Heart attack: The death of heart cells due to lack of oxygen.

Heredity: The passing on of traits from parent to offspring.

Hybrid: The combination of nonidentical gene pairs.

Hyperthermia: Excessively high body temperature.

Hypothalamus: A small part of the brain that monitors automatic functions, such as pulse rate, temperature of the blood, sweating, and shivering.

Hypothermia: Excessively low body temperature.

Identical twins: The result when one ovum is fertilized and the dividing zygote splits in two, and each half develops into a baby.

Impulses: Electric signals that travel from one neuron to another.

Incisors: Knife-shaped teeth in the front of the mouth that cut and slice food.

Inertia: The tendency of an object to remain stationary or to continue to move unless acted on by an outside force.

Inhale: To breathe in, bringing gases into the lungs.

Inherited traits: Traits passed on through heredity.

Inspiration: Movement of air into the lungs.

Intensity: The amount of energy used per second.

Involuntary movements: Body movements that happen without your controlling them, such as the beating of your heart.

Iris: The visible, colored muscular curtain in the front of the eye which is part of the choroid.

Joint: The place where bones meet.

Keratin: A tough protein found in skin, nails, and hair.

Large intestine: The tubular organ where water is taken out of digested food and the remains temporarily stored until they are passed from the body as waste.

Larynx: The voice box.

Lens: The part of the eye that focuses light on the fovea.

Ligaments: Tough, straplike strands of connective tissue that hold bones together.

"Lock-and-key" theory: The belief that odors are identified when their molecules fit into the cells of chemoreceptors, just as a key fits into a lock.

Luna: White half-moon shaped area at the base of the nail, where the growth of the nail takes place.

Lysosomes: The parts of the cell that contain chemicals used to destroy harmful substances or worn-out cells parts.

Macula (plural **maculae**):   Special sensory area inside the utricle and saccule that contains otoliths.

Mechanoreceptor: A sensory receptor that is stimulated by pressure, touch, or sound.

Medulla: A part of the brain that is located at the base of the cerebrum and connected to the top of the spinal cord;

controls involuntary movements, such as the beating of your heart.

Melanin: Special cells containing dark grains that produce skin color.

Metabolism: All the chemical and physical processes of the body.

Mitochondria (singular **mitochondrion**): The cell's power stations where food and oxygen react to produce the energy needed for the cell to work and live.

Mnemonic devices: Ways of organizing material to help you remember it quickly and easily.

Molars: Grinding teeth on each side of the mouth that mash food and mix it with saliva.

Molecule: The smallest particle of a substance.

Motor neurons: Nerve cells that carry impulses to muscles and other parts of the body.

Mucus: A sticky, slippery liquid that lines the organs of the breathing and digestive systems.

Nail root: The part of the skin from which finger- and toe-nails grow.

Nerves: Special fibers that the body uses to send messages to and from the brain and spinal cord.

Neurons: Nerve cells.

Nociceptor: A sensory receptor that is stimulated by pain.

Noise level: The intensity of a sound compared with the quietest sound the ear can hear.

Nucleus: The control center that directs all the activities of the cell.

Nutrients: Microscopic building blocks produced by the digestion of food and used by the cells for growth, repair, and energy.

Optic nerve: The main nerve connecting the eye to the brain.

Organ: A group of different tissues working together to perform a job, such as the heart, lungs, or stomach.

Organism: All the systems working together in a living being.

Osmosis: The movement of water through a cell membrane from the side that has more water to the side that has less water.

Ossicles: The three tiny bones in the inner ear called the hammer, the anvil, and the stirrup.

Otoliths: Tiny calcium carbonate crystals found in maculae that are moved by gravity and that detect the position of the head.

Oval window: The membrane that covers the entrance to the inner ear.

Ovaries: The pair of female organs where ova are produced.

Ovum (plural **ova**): Female sex cell, or egg.

Oxygen: A colorless gas in the air that is needed by every cell in the body.

Papillae: Groups of taste buds.

Periosteum: The thin, tough outer layer of bones.

Peristalsis: Waves of muscle contractions inside the body to move substances along. Food moves through the esophagus and intestines by peristalsis.

Pharynx: The throat.

Photoreceptor: A sensory receptor that is stimulated by visible light.

Pitch: Highness or lowness of sound.

Placenta: A special organ that serves as a barrier separating the baby's blood from the mother's blood, and through which the baby receives nourishment and oxygen and wastes are removed.

Plasma: The clear yellow liquid that makes up about 55 percent of blood.

Platelets: Tiny fragments of blood cells, which aid in the process of blood clotting.

Posterior: Situated behind.

Pregnancy: The condition of carrying an unborn baby.

Pulse: Throbbing heartbeat felt strongly in the arteries close to the skin's surface, such as in the wrist.

Punnett square: A method of showing all the possible gene combinations that are transferred from parents to offspring.

Pupil: The black dot-like opening in the center of the iris that is dilated or constricted by the muscles of the iris.

Pure traits: The combination of identical gene pairs.

Recessive gene: A gene that does not determine the trait of the offspring when a dominant gene is present.

Reflex: An automatic response to a stimulus that is made without the brain's direct involvement.

Refracted: Bent. Refraction is a change of the direction of light that passes through the lens of the eye.

Respiration: The process by which oxygen combines with glucose to produce energy and two waste byproducts, carbon dioxide, and water vapor.

Retina: The expanded end of the optic nerve that makes up the inside layer of the eyeball. It contains rods and cones, and is the location of the fovea.

Rod: A light-sensitive cell in the eye that detects black-and-white images.

Saccule: Tiny fluid-filled sac in the inner ear that detects motion of the body.

Saliva: Liquid in the mouth that softens and partially digests food.

Scab: The hardened blood clot on the surface of the skin.

Sclera: The tough outer covering of the eye that forms what is called the "whites" of the eye.

Sebum: Natural oil that covers the skin with a film.

Semicircular canals: Three fluid-filled, curved passages in the inner ear, which help to maintain balance.

Semipermeable membrane: A cell membrane that allows only certain sized particles to pass through it. The holes are large enough to admit water but too small to admit many larger particles.

Sensory neurons: Nerve cells that carry impulses from sensory receptors in areas such as your eyes, nose, and skin to the spinal cord.

Sensory receptors: Cells that receive stimuli of sight, hearing, smell, taste, and touch.

Septum: A muscular wall separating the right and left sides of the heart.

Sexual reproduction: The process of producing a new organism from two parents.

Shivering: The contraction of skeletal muscles to produce body heat; controlled by the hypothalamus.

Skeletal system: All the bones of the body, which together provide a supportive and protective framework.

Small intestine: The long tubular organ of the digestive system where nutrients pass into the bloodstream.

Sneeze: The action by which the body removes irritating particles from the nose by forcing a burst of air out of the lungs through the nose at a speed of up to about 100 miles (161 km) per hour.

Soft palate: The back part of the roof of the mouth which moves up and closes off the nasal passage during swallowing.

Solution: A mixture of water and dissolved particles of a substance.

Sound waves: Vibrations traveling through the air.

Sperm: Male sex cell.

Sphincter: A muscle between the stomach and duodenum that relaxes and contracts to open and close the entrance from the stomach to the duodenum.

Spinal canal: The passageway of holes in the back parts of the vertebrae through which the spinal cord is threaded.

Spinal cord: The large bundle of nerves running down through the spine from the medulla.

Stimulated: Excited.

Stimulus (plural **stimuli**):   Something that temporarily excites or quickens a response.

Stomach: The part of the digestive system where the bolus is churned into small pieces and mixed with gastric juices, which change the solid food to liquid.

Sweat: Liquid produced by sweat glands that contains mostly water with dissolved salts and other substances.

System: A group of different organs working together to perform a particular job; for example, the circulatory system.

Taste buds: Chemoreceptors found abundantly on the tongue, and sparsely on the soft palate and in the throat, that are responsible for the sense of taste.

Tendon: Tough, ropy tissue that connects muscle to bone.

Thermoreceptor: A sensory receptor that is stimulated by heat and cold.

Tissue: A group of similar cells that perform a special job.

Trachea: The tube through which air passes on the way to the lungs, which is also called the windpipe.

Traits: Characteristics that help to identify living organisms, such as hair color, eye color, and height.

Transparent: See-through or clear.

Tympanic membrane: The eardrum.

Umbilical cord: The flexible tissue that connects the placenta to the fetus.

Unconditioned reflex: A reflex that does not depend on previous experience.

Uterus: Organ of the female body where the baby grows and develops.

Utricle: Tiny fluid-filled sac in the inner ear that detects motion of the body.

Vagina: The passageway between the uterus and the outside of the female body.

Valve: A flap in veins that allows blood to flow in one direction only.

Veins: Blood vessels that carry blood back to the heart.

Ventricle: One of the two lower chambers of the heart.

Vertebra (plural **vertebrae**): One of the 26 bones that make up your spine.

Vibrate: To move to and fro.

Vocal cords: Two strips of tough, elastic tissue and muscle stretched across the opening of the larynx. Air passing over the vocal cords makes them vibrate and produce sounds.

Voluntary movements: Body movements that you can control, such as raising your arm.

Water vapor: Water in the form of gas.

Zygote: Fertilized egg.

Index